William Thomas, James Anthony Froude

The Pilgrim

A Dialogue on the Life and Actions of King Henry the Eighth

William Thomas, James Anthony Froude

The Pilgrim

A Dialogue on the Life and Actions of King Henry the Eighth

ISBN/EAN: 9783337290030

Printed in Europe, USA, Canada, Australia, Japan

Cover: Foto ©Suzi / pixelio.de

More available books at **www.hansebooks.com**

THE PILGRIM.

THE PILGRIM:

A DIALOGUE

ON THE

LIFE AND ACTIONS OF KING HENRY THE EIGHTH.

BY

WILLIAM THOMAS,
CLERK OF THE COUNCIL TO EDWARD VI.

EDITED, WITH NOTES FROM THE ARCHIVES AT PARIS AND BRUSSELS,

BY

J. A. FROUDE,
AUTHOR OF "THE HISTORY OF ENGLAND, FROM THE FALL OF WOLSEY TO THE DEATH OF ELIZABETH."

LONDON:
PARKER, SON, AND BOURN, WEST STRAND.
1861.

LONDON:
SAVILL AND EDWARDS, PRINTERS, CHANDOS STREET,
COVENT GARDEN.

PREFACE.

WHEN I wrote the early volumes of my History of England this book was unknown to me. I was aware that a defence of Henry the Eighth had been written after his death by a clerk of the Privy Council; but from the short mention of the thing by Strype, I could learn little either of its character or value; nor was I aware that a copy survived till I encountered one by accident among the Harleian MSS. in the British Museum. Subsequently, I met with a second copy among the Lansdowne MSS.; and later still, I found that the book was printed in the last century among a collection of tracts by the same author.

The printed edition, however, is so rare that for purposes of reference it is scarcely more accessible than the MSS. I do not doubt that to the large majority of English readers the book will be as new as it was to me, and I believe myself to be doing useful service in bringing it again before the world.

The outward events of the reign of Henry the Eighth are patent and acknowledged. The question, so far as question exists, is of the causes in which those events originated. The Statute Book gives one account of those causes; popular tradition gives another. The opinion of a contemporary English gentleman, who had no object to gain by dishonest advocacy, cannot but contribute something towards a just decision between the two authorities.

To those who find an adequate explanation of the Acts of Parliament in the cowardice and servility of the Lords and Commons I put a question to which no answer has ever been given or attempted. What means had Henry the Eighth at his disposal to compel their compliance or punish their disobedience? He had a mere handful of men, whose number he never attempted to increase. The Council, under Edward the Sixth, found it necessary to surround themselves with a 'Gendarmerie;' Queen Mary's incessant effort was to have a military force at her private disposal; Henry the Eighth was contented with the yeomen of the guard, who might have been scattered by a rising of the apprentices. Except for the voluntary loyalty of his subjects, half-a-dozen noblemen might at any moment have overturned the throne. The House of Commons when called on to stamp themselves with ignominy by sanctioning Anne Boleyn's execution, need but have adjourned in a body from Westminster to Whitehall to have the King their prisoner.

It has been said that to find a difficulty in the acquiescence of the Parliament is to betray an ignorance of the histories of other reigns of terror. I reply that the annals of the world contain no record of a reign of terror conducted under such extraordinary conditions. The English were no mob of helpless peasants; they were a nation of soldiers, fierce, intractable, and turbulent to a proverb. London alone contained a drilled force of twenty thousand men at the disposal of the corporation; and so far was the King from showing a wish to disarm the people, that more than once at different periods of his reign, he forced the whole strength of England into the field, and himself with but a handful of servants rode up and down along the highways amidst thousands of armed men. If not contented with indulging in private his abominable passions, he had insulted Peers and Commons, Catholics and Protestants, with requiring them to disguise his crimes under a hypocritical aspect of justice, his long impunity is a phenomenon inconceivably marvellous. Our boasted parliamentary government and trial by jury are but poor securities for justice if they could be tortured into instruments of tyranny by means so feeble.

I speak generally of the broad hypothesis of servility which has been employed to cover the whole complications of this reign. They require far subtler and more delicate explanation. Cruel deeds were done; but they were done by the alternating influences of the two great parties in the State, to whom nothing was wrong which furthered their separate objects. The King himself was rather the moderator than the instigator when either Protestants suffered as heretics, or Catholics as traitors; and deeds, which both sides alike must have known and acknowledged to be enormous crimes, I see no reason either to believe the King guilty of perpetrating, or the Parliament of permitting or sanctioning.

At all events, those who are capable of understanding the difficulties of the popular view will welcome an opportunity of seeing the conduct of Henry the Eighth as it appeared to an Englishman of more than common ability, who himself witnessed the scenes which he describes.

The history of the writer is soon told. He was by birth a Welshman, and was brought up at Oxford. Towards the end of Henry's reign he was obliged to leave England, perhaps for his religious opinions; and repairing to Italy he composed among other things an Italian grammar. He returned home the year of Edward the Sixth's accession, when he was appointed clerk of the Council, and became a sort of political instructor of the young King. Without the knowledge of the Government, he seems to have secretly given Edward lessons on the principles of government, on the state of the currency and similar questions; and his teaching, if not his hand, is perceptible in the King's journal. When Edward died, he attached himself to the Protestant party. He took part in Wyatt's conspiracy, and died in May, 1554, at Tyburn.

It was while he was at Bologna, two months after Henry's death, that, (if the form of *The Pilgrim* is more than a fiction,) the conversation took place which gave rise to the composition of the book. The internal evidence shows at any rate that it was written while the author was still on the Continent. He did not publish it; there was no occasion for a defence of Henry in England while the recollection of him was fresh and before the Italian views of his character had naturalized themselves; later in the century, in a changed era of men and things, Elizabeth's position must have forbidden the appearance of a production which reflected so hardly on her mother.

Such as the book is, it will speak for itself. It is not free from mistakes. The writer knew many things which we have no means of knowing. By the production of secret papers we, on our part, know some things which he could not know. His story has the accuracies and the inaccuracies which we might naturally look for in any account of a series of intricate events given by memory without the assistance of documents. It has the value which an account would have if given by any able middle-aged man now living, of the first war with China, for instance, of the war with Russia, the Irish famine, or the political struggles in Parliament during the last fifteen years. The particulars of such an account would be often inexact, but the outline and effect would represent the impression generally current in the country; and in that way, and to that degree, I believe the writer of *The Pilgrim* to represent to us the popular view of the conduct and character of Henry the Eighth, as received in England at the time of his death.

So much for the book. I must add a few words about the notes.

When for the story in the Statute Book is claimed the support of the recently examined State Papers, it is replied, that being the work of the same hands, there is no wonder if they tell the same story.

The answer is not strictly to the point; because,

under the term State Papers, are comprised not merely official letters or statements, but miscellaneous reports of the most varied kind; depositions of witnesses on trials; examinations of accused persons; accounts of private conversations; or of casual expressions dropped in church or on highway, in private house or public hostelry.

But it is true that all the State Records passed through the hands of the ministers of the day. If they did not forge what made in their favour, they had opportunities of destroying what made against them. The records of the trial of Catherine Howard are perfect; the records of the trial of Anne Boleyn survive only in a faint epitome; and we know neither by whom nor why the evidence was made away with. The support of disinterested testimony is therefore of more value to the reputation of the statesmen whose conduct is called in question, than any document which they left behind in their own portfolios; and the testimony of enemies must be weighed beside the testimony of friends.

From William Thomas we hear the best which could be said for Henry by an ordinary unofficial Englishman. I desired to hear the worst also—the worst, I mean, which could be said at the time by men who knew him, of actions passing under their eyes—and this object I have endeavoured to obtain from the despatches of the French and Imperial ambassadors resident at the English Court. French, Spaniards, and Flemings were alike Catholics, and alike regarded the revolt from the See of Rome as an enormous crime. The Spaniards had received mortal affront in the divorce of Queen Catherine; the French Court was the training-school, the French Sovereign the patron, of Anne Boleyn. Neither d'Inteville, Chastillon, nor Marillac, neither Mendoza nor Eustace Chappuys were men to let their eyes be blinded in Henry's favour: and in their safe and cyphered correspondence with their own Governments, they would throw no pleasant veil over a series of crimes and scandals.

With a view, therefore, of seeing Henry in the least favourable aspect, I have spent some part of this past summer among the Archives of Paris and Brussels. The result will be found in the notes of this present volume.

I have not found all that I desired. The correspondence of d'Inteville, the French minister, for instance, continues to within a month of Anne Boleyn's arrest; it recommences a month after her execution; and the letters in which the story of that tragedy was told were either destroyed, to stifle the recollection of it, or were set apart from their especial interest, and now are lost.

On the other hand, I have found many things for which I did not look. The materials are abundant, and from the mass of letters I have been obliged to content myself with extracts.

I believe, however, that I have omitted nothing of importance; certainly, I have omitted nothing knowingly which tells in the King's disfavour.

The letters at Paris are in French. The letters at Brussels in French, Spanish, and Latin. After some hesitation what I ought to do, and being certain that do what I would I could not please every one, I have studied the convenience of the majority of my readers, and have rendered them all into English.

My original copies are at the service of any one who will give me good reason for wishing to see them.

Castigans castigavit me Dominus,
Et morti non tradidit me.—W. T.

To Mr. Peter Aretine, *the Right Natural Poet.*

LIKE as many times the wild woods and barren mountains yield more delight unto the seldom-travelled Citizen than do the pleasant orchards and gardens, whose beauty and fruit he daily enjoyeth, so hath it now pleased me rather to direct this my little book unto thee, whose virtue consisteth only in Nature without any art, than unto any other; whom I know both natural, virtuous, and learned withal: specially because I understand that the King, in defence of whose honour I have made it, hath remembered thee with an honourable legacy* by his Testament; the which his enemies pretend proceeded from the fear that he had lest thou shouldest, after his death, defame him with thy wonted ill speech. But to let them wit that no man with right can slander him, and to open also unto them part of his worthy and glorious doings, whereof, if thou wilt, thou mayst fully speak unto his great honour, I have in this little book briefly declared the most part of such successes as have

---

* No legacy was left by Henry VIII. to Pietro Aretino.

happened unto him in his lifetime, with the occasions that thereunto moved me, and have thought good to participate the same unto thee, to the intent that if any person should repugn against it, thou, with the mountain of thy natural reasons, shouldest have matter sufficient accordingly to defend it; in which doing Thou shalt partly satisfy both unto the very truth, and also unto the good memory that so noble a King hath deserved of thee.

                    Farewell.

                             W. T.

A Relation of a Conference had between WILLIAM THOMAS, *Clerk of the Council to* KING EDWARD VI., *and certain Italian Gentlemen in his Travels, touching the Actions of* KING HENRY VIII., *entitled* PEREGRINE. Anno 1546.

> He that dieth with honour liveth for ever,
> And the defamed dead recovereth never.

CONSTRAINED by misfortune to abandon the place of my nativity, and to walk at the random of the wide world; in the month of February, and after the Church of England the year of our Lord God 1546, it happened me to arrive in the city of Bonony in the region of Italy; where, in company of certain gentlemen, known to be an Englishman, I was earnestly apposed of the nature, quality, and customs of my country, and especially of divers particular things touching the estate of our King's Majesty Henry the 8th, who then nearly was departed out of this present life. And albeit that my gross intelligence extended not to the sufficient satisfaction of those important questions that were there demanded of me, yet, to avoid occasioning of discourtesy towards those courteous gentlemen who so courteously provoked me, and to learn of them some notable things worth the knowledge (and being, as they were, men of singular reputation and judgment), I enterprised liberally to commune with them and to say mine opinion touching the things in question. The discourse whereof I have thought good to put in writing, not only for the private defence of that noble Prince whose honour hath been wrongfully touched, but also for the general satisfaction of them whose ears may happen to be occupied with unjust and false rumours; beseeching thee, therefore, gentle reader, to accept the truth of mine intent without offence, in case thine appetite should move thee to mislike my report : for, surely, if thou set apart affection to govern thee with the discourse of reason, thou shalt also perceive that mine answer proceeds more of pure simplicity than of prepensed malice, in that part specially that excuseth the blamed doings of my foresaid King, who in his lifetime was much more able indeed to justify himself against all the world, than I now after his death am able to defend him with my pen.

After supper on an evening, sitting by the fire in company of seven or eight gentlemen in a rich merchant's house in Bonony, among other things, when they had reasoned of many matters, their whole talk fell upon me, by occasion of the King who then was newly departed this world. And there was it first asked me of what circuit might the whole isle of England be; whereunto I answered, that after the description of Cosmography it did extend in compass upon the points to 2000 Italian miles; but in this, said I, you must understand Scotland to be comprehended.

'And what may Scotland contain?' said one of them.

'I think,' said I, 'that Scotland may be somewhat better than as it were a fourth part of the island.'

'And how is the country's fertility?' said he.

I answered, ' that it was abundant of grain and cattle; and to compare it unto Italy, I shall tell you what difference there is. Here, in Italy, groweth wine, oil, and divers sorts of fruits that grow not with us; as melons, pippins, pomegranates, oranges, figs, raisins, and some other such; because the cold air of our country cannot nourish them, being, as we are, six degrees further from the sun than you be. But instead of these your commodities—first, for wine, we have great abundance of barley, whereof our ale and beer are made, which, for our common drink, agreeth better with our nature than the continual drinkings of wine should do. And then for oil, we have so much sweet butter, that though well we had abundance thereof as you have, yet, think I, there be few that would use it in their meats as you do; since butter pleaseth our appetites much better than oil. And in that you exceed us in fruits, we exceed you both in the abundance, and also in the goodness, of flesh, fowl, and fish, whereof the common people there do no less feed than your common people here of herbs and fruits. And again, for wines, we have continually from France and Spain, as also out of Almaine and out of Candia, great quantity of the best that grow in those parts, and of oil and all those other fruits that are rehearsed, the melon only excepted. It is true that we pay dear for them, and that we have not such plenty as you have : nor, to say the truth, we need it not; for like as the subtle air of Italy doth not allow you to feed grossly, so the gross air of England doth not allow us to feed subtilely. Here the temperate heat requireth food of light digestion, as fruits, herbs, little flesh and delicate diet; and there the temperate cold requireth food of more substance, as abundance of flesh and fish, which satisfy the appetite; and thereof groweth the proverb—Give the Englyshman beoffe and mustarde.'

'Yea, but what meaneth it,' said they, 'that your nation supporteth no strangers, as by daily proof it is right well seen? When an outlandish man passeth by, you call him whoreson knave, dog, and other like. This seemeth unto us a very barbarous part.'

'I shall tell you why,' said I. 'In times past, our nation hath practised as little abroad in strange countries as any nation of the world; and the commodities of our country are so great that the ignorant persons, seeing strangers resort unto them for traffic, and, as it is true, for gain, imagined they came not to buy their commodities, but to rob them, and that they who so used to traffic, for lack of living in their own countries, applied the merchandize of England as of necessity. But at this day it is all otherwise; for like as your merchants do practise in England, so our merchants do now traffic abroad, and by travel have attained such knowledge of civility that I warrant you those strangers who now repair into England are as well received and seen, and as much made of as in any other kingdom of all Europe, especially in the

Prince's Court, and among the nobles, where surely hath evermore been seen all honour and courtesy.'

'We believe you,' said they; 'but those commodities that you speak of, what be they?'

'Beside the abundant meat,' said I, 'there groweth in England great quantity of wool, the finest of all the world, whereof the kerseys and broad-cloths of London are made; and all the fine cloths which are called *panni diffiandra* are also English cloths wrong named by reason of the mart at Antwerp in Flanders, where these cloths are most commonly bought and sold. Then have we leather, whereof continually goeth out of the realm a marvellous quantity, a good witness of the great abundance of cattle that the country doth nourish. We have also mines of lead, tin, and, in some places, of silver; but the silver veins do prove so slender that in manner it yieldeth not the miner's charge, so that it is left unsought for. But the lead and tin prove so abundant that there is continually bought and sold out of the realm great quantities thereof. Then have we mines of natural coal.'

'What mean you by natural coal?' said they.

'Natural coal,' said I, 'is a certain black substance of the earth, congealed in veins, as other metals be, serving to none other purpose but to burn only, which in the burning yieldeth a much greater heat than doth the wood coal, and after that it is burned, consumeth not into ashes, but resteth hard as a stone. So that because it serveth much better for the smith's occupation than doth the other coal, there is yearly sold out of the realm a great quantity thereof unto Dutchland, Flanders, and France. And another notable commodity we have; whether the cause be in our industry or in the goodness of our waters, I cannot tell; the Flemings do buy much of our beer, because it is better than theirs, and pay almost as much for it as we do to the Frenchmen for their wine. And, finally, divers other commodities there be of smaller moment, too long now to rehearse.'

'Yea,' said one of them, 'that drunken beer it is that fatteneth the Flemings like hogs. But surely these your commodities rehearsed are very notable, and I marvel not, though your Island be rich and wealthy (as it is reported), seeing that it hath so many means to draw money into it, when on the other side that money that cometh into your hands can never be had out again; for your King hath kept the passage so straitly that no man could carry out of the realm in ready money above 10 ducats; so that it is no marvel,' said he, 'though he had mountains of gold, as they say he had.'

'No,' said another of them, 'that law is finished. It is true that whilst the English money was better than other money, no man, as you say, could carry it away; but now that the said King, for his own private gain, hath made it worse than any other money, each man may carry away so much as him liketh.'

'Why,' said I, ' can ye blame him to take his advantage as all other Princes do? See you not that all the gold and silver is abased in all the new money that is now made anywhere? I suppose he should have been reported a very simple man to have holden up his fine money for a bait when other men's money decayed; and, as touching the Prince's gain (how well in common I cannot see where any man thereby sustaineth any loss), I think he did better to gain so upon his own money, than, as other Princes do, to borrow so of their private subjects and never pay.'

'What!' said that other unto me, 'you are earnest in your King's favour; but you consider not that Cicero his eloquence should not suffice to defend him of his tyranny, since he hath been known, and noted over all, to be the greatest tyrant that ever was in England.'

'In this case,' said I, 'you charge my patience, and the answer of so outrageous a report requireth more force than reason or writing. But, because the place alloweth me not to speak, much less to fight, I therefore will forbear. But tell me, I pray you, have you ever been in England?'

'No,' said he, 'but in Picardy I have been, and also in Flanders, where by report I have known all the proceedings in England, and known them so well that in every point I should be well able to defend both with reason and force against you, not only that I have said, but much more, if need were. But because I am an Italian, and you a stranger, your brags shall have place for this time.'

At the which words, somewhat troubled in my mind, I sought leave to depart; but the other gentlemen present held me by force, and would in any wise hear that matter resolutely disputed; insomuch that, having moved my Contrary to allege against the King's Majesty what he could say, they temperately persuaded me to answer, to the intent it might appear who had the wrong. And thus both parties quieted, after a little pause, seeming rather to have studied this matter than to have conceived it by hearing-say, this gentleman, my Contrary, thus began his argument.

'If you,' said he, 'will grant me that the principal token of a tyrant is the immoderate satisfaction of an unlawful appetite, when the person, whether by right or wrong, hath power to achieve his sensual will, and that the person, also, who by force draweth unto him that which of right is not his, in the unlawful usurping committeth express tyranny; then doubt I not right well to justify my report with advantage.

'1. Your King his first wife, I pray you, being the Emperor's aunt, did he not cast her off after that he had lived in lawful matrimony with her 18 years?

'2. And to acccomplish his will in the new marriage of his second wife, because Pope Clement would not consent to him, did he not disannul the authority of the Holy Roman Church, which for long time hath been honoured and obeyed of all Christian Princes?

'3. Thirdly—Because the Cardinal of Rochester, and Thomas More, High Chancellor of England, would not allow these his abominable errors, did he not cause them to be beheaded? men whose famous doctrine hath merited eternal memory; and when he had rid them out of the world, who only with learning and reason were able to resist his beastly appetite.

'4. Did he not presume to take on him the Papal title and authority; disposing bishoprics and benefices of the Church as Christ's Vicar on earth; like as it is manifest he did unto his dying day?

'5. The poor St. Thomas of Canterbury, alas! it sufficed him not to spoil and devour the great riches of the shrine, whose treasure amounted to so many thousand crowns; but, to be avenged on the dead corpse, did he not cause his bones openly to be burned?

'6. And, consequently, all the places where God by his saints vouchsafed to show so many miracles, did he not cause them to be spoiled of their riches, jewels, and ornaments, and after clean destroyed, nor would not so much as suffer in those few churches that remained the light to burn before the images of God's most holy saints?

'7. The monasteries wherein God was continually served, did he not overthrow them, and take all their riches and possessions unto his own use; crucifying and tormenting the poor religious persons even unto the death, with whose goods he became more puissant in gold than any Christian Prince?

'8. After the insurrection in the North, when he had pardoned the first rebellers against him, contrary unto his promise did he not cause a number of the most noble of them, by divers torments, to be put to death?

'9. And not his first wife, but three or four more, did he not chop, change, and behead them, as his horse coveted new pasture, to satisfy the inordinate appetite of his lecherous will? Two of his wives he hath caused suffer death, and two remain yet alive.

'10. Did he not persecute the Cardinal Pole, whose virtue and learning seemeth rare unto the world? And hath he not wrongfully murdered the Cardinal's mother, his brother, and so many other nobles that it should all be too long to rehearse?

'11. He hath by force subdued the realm of Ireland, whereunto he hath neither right nor title; and wasted, he hath, no small part of Scotland, with intent to subdue the whole without cause or reason.

'12. Against all conscience, he hath moved war unto France, and by force usurped the strong town of Bollogne, which he keepeth unto this hour.

'13. His daughter, the Lady Mary, that he had by his first wife, being one of the fairest, the most virtuous, and one of the gentlest creatures in all the world, is now grown to the age of thirty-two or thirty-three years, and, through his devilish obstinacy, could never be married.

'14. And, finally, to finish his cruel life with bloody rage, now, a little before his death, hath he not beheaded the old Duke of Norfolk with his son, for what cause no man can tell? So that I wot not what Nero, what Dionysius, or what Mahomet may be compared unto him, in whom, towards God, rested no reverence of religion, nor, towards man, no kind of compassion; whose sword, inflamed by continual heat of innocent blood, and whose bottomless belly could never be satisfied through the throat of extreme avarice and rapine; whose inconstant mind, occupied with occasion of continual war, permitted not his quiet neighbours to live in peace; and, in conclusion, whose unreasonable will had place alway and in all things, against all equity and reason. Ah! if I would go about to declare at length the particular enormities that I have heard reported against him, a part whereof I have briefly recited unto you, I should give occasion of trouble to a whole world! But since this that I have said, is, I doubt not, sufficient to justify my purpose, I have thought it better with few words to let you know how manifest his tyranny was, than with long circumstance to occupy your quiet mind with the terror of so much cruelty as I could justly allege. Answer me now, who that will, for I am tired, not with talk, but with the remembrance of so many mischiefs as this reasoning representeth to my conscience: and yet one thing I have to say; your King, being environed with the ocean sea, thought it impossible that the fame of his wicked life and doings should pass unto the firm land of other countries; and therefore the more hardily did enterprise the fulfilling of his devilish desires. But in that behalf he was no less deceived than blinded in his own errors; for not only his general proceedings, but also every particular and private part thereof was better known in Italy than in his own dominions, where, for fear, no man durst either speak or wink.'

And thus having finished his heavy and fervent talk, he gave me place of speech. But I, who in this sudden case was not so promptly prepared with distinct answers to satisfy the company as he thus roundly had charged me, rested in manner amazed; partly because meseemed the other gentlemen inclined towards a certain credit of his report, and partly also for fear of the place wherein I found myself. For Bonony (though well with wrong) is of the Pope's territory, and he that speaketh there against the Pope incurreth no less danger than he that in England would offend the King's Majesty. Insomuch that one of them, perceiving me so oppressed with an inward passion, very courteously encouraged me to defend the cause that I had taken in hand, without respect of fear. So that after I had told him that, without the Pope's offence, I could not make my reason good, which the presence of the place prohibited me—assured of them all, in one voice, to speak at liberty what I would, without danger or displeasure, all joyfully imagining the victory in hand, I thus began to say :—

'Universally in all things do I find one singular and perfect rule, which is this, that the outward appearance is always preferred before the inward existence, and that most commonly do all things otherwise appear to be than as they are indeed. As for example, the fair woman (of him that by love seeketh to rejoice her) is rather regarded for her outward beauty than for her inward virtue; and many times under the veil of a smiling face is covered the poison of a cankered heart. Yea, and when I had no other proof unto this my purpose, but that all living men are known to bear more earnest love unto the presence of these vain earthy riches, than to the hidden infinite virtue of the everlasting God the Creator, I think the same only should suffice to declare how ignorant that man's common judgment is, as long as it is occupied with the appearance of the thing, and penetrateth not into the essential substance, as in this our present matter you shall right well perceive it hath happened. For the person that will only regard the argument that the gentleman here hath, with the particular witness of those things that he hath rehearsed, which, in part, are surely true, and discern no further, he, I say, must rest undoubtedly persuaded that the deceased King was no less than a cruel tyrant, by reason that in all things it should seem he followed more his unlawful appetite than any reasonable virtue. But, on the other side, he that will pass through the outward discourse and recur unto the inward occasion, how, why, and in what manner these things have succeeded, shall clearly find the effect to contain all another reason than it seemeth to do; as mine answer to his oppositions by one and one, shall, I doubt not, prove sufficiently; nothing mistrusting at all, but that they who covet the light of the truth shall receive singular pleasure in hearing me. Wherefore, I shall heartily beseech you of quiet audience unto the full declaration of my purpose. And yet, or ever it shall become me to dispute in so weighty a cause, Reason commendeth me to know both the nature and religion of the person whom it behoveth me to answer; so that (said I unto my Contrary), I shall pray you not to disdain to tell me what is your profession and what your religion: as for your quality, I nothing doubt but that you are gentleman, for so doth your port and gesture sufficiently assure me.'

'As for that,' said he, 'I will not make it strange. My profession is to serve the wars, though well I live upon my lands; and my religion is to believe in the Holy Mother Church, as my father and all mine ancestors have done.'

'Very well,' said I; 'in the whole is evermore comprehended the part, and therefore unto the particular, which, as I can remember, dependeth thirteen or fourteen several points, I answer that first, as touching the divorce had between the King's Majesty to the Lady Katherine, his first wife, which was the Emperor's aunt, it is to be considered whether in that behalf his Highness's intent was to proceed lawfully or unlawfully, privily or openly; for commonwealth or his own personal commodity; in the trial of which three distinctions the matter must appear. And thus standeth the case.

'The King's Majesty deceased, in the time of his father Henry the 7th, had an elder brother named Arthur, heir apparent to the crown of England, unto whom this Lady Katherine was first married. Whether they coupled in natural knowledge or not God knoweth, for unto me it appertaineth not to judge, but they were of lawful age. Now, sir, this Prince Arthur died before the father, and during the father's life this lady remained a widow; but incontinently as the father was dead and the King that now is departed came to the crown, his Majesty became enamoured in her, both because of her rare beauty and also for her singular virtues, which seemed then more to flourish in her than in any other living woman. But because the law of God in Christ permitteth not the brother to enjoy the brother's wife, as the especial proof of Herod, whom John Baptist therefore rebuked, doth well declare, his Highness, as for extreme remedy unto his unlawful case, recurred unto the Pope's dispensation, believing at that time (as many yet do believe) the same to be of much more effect than God's commandments. And so having unto great suit and for extreme sums of money at length obtained superstitious licence, he attempted the act of matrimony, and quietly lived, as you have said, with the Lady Katherine eighteen years or thereabouts ; having issue by her that gentle Lady Mary, whose beauty and virtue you have most worthily commended. But when the time came that God opened his Majesty's eyes and spirit to consider this his unlawful act, not trusting yet altogether unto the divine inspiration of the spirit, how well divers of his prudent and learned counsellors had persuaded him plainly that the matter could not stand well, he nevertheless sent first unto Rome unto Clement the 7th for the resolution of his judgment in that behalf; praying him, if the matter appeared unlawful before God, to grant him not only a divorce, but also a licence to marry again, for divers good and Christian respects.

'But Clement, smiling in his heart at so meet an occasion, and thinking of this rich King to shear such another golden fleece as Jason conquered in Colchis, threw forth so weak a training-bait that the great fish swallowed his hook and broke his line. For straightway sent he the Cardinal Campeggio, legate a latere, into England to determine this matter ; who, sitting there in judgment, had such courage of presumption that he caused the King, as a private person, to appear before him, and the Lady Katherine both ; and there was this matter so long disputed *pro et contra*, that finally, not only the civil and moral laws, but also by the Pope's self canon laws the commandment of God had place and the error of the Pope's dispensation was discovered; so that, in conclusion, his Majesty was divorced from the said Lady Katherine, not unlawfully by extorted power, either of the King himself or of any of his subjects, but lawfully by the true examination of the verity before such a judge as coveted rather to rule the King than to obey him: and it cannot be said that he did it privily, for all the world was present to the matter in question more than twenty months or ever it took effect.*

'And then as for his personal commodity, I think no man so ignorant but that he may consider how that he always might have had secretly at his pleasure numbers of fair women—England being, as it were, replenished with the fairest creatures of the world. But he did it first with reverence to God, whose commandment each creature is bound to obey, and after the commonwealth of his realm, the inhabitants whereof are of all other most inclinable to sedition upon every least occasion; so that in time to come, whensoever any great man should have rebelled against the royal blood, alleging the King's children in their case not to be born in lawful matrimony, it should have been like enough to have moved mortal civil war, as small occasions in times past have yielded manifest proof; whereas now having had by the undoubted Queen Jane, his lawful wife, a most gracious son named Edward,

---

* See Note A. p. 83.

who lawfully hath received the crown, the whole realm must needs persevere in happy peace and joy. And therefore methinketh him much to blame that for so reasonable a doing would defame so circumspect a prince.

'2. Now unto that you say that because Pope Clement would not dispense with this second matrimony, his Majesty extirpted out of England the Papal authority, a thing of most ancient and godly reverence as you take it; I answer, that after the King's Highness had so appeared in person before the Cardinal Campeggio, one of the princes of his realm, named the Duke of Suffolk, a great wise man, and of more familiarity with the King than any other person, asked his Majesty how this matter might come to pass that a Prince in his own realm should so humble himself before the feet of a vile, strange, vicious priest (for Campeggio there in England demeaned himself in very deed most carnally in hunting of whores, playing at dice and cards, and sundry such other cardinal exercises), whereto the King answered, he could not tell, but only that it seemed unto him that spiritual men ought to judge spiritual matters. 'And yet, as you say,' said the King, 'meseemeth there should be somewhat in it; and I could right gladly understand why and how, were it not that I would be loth to appear more curious than other Princes.' 'Why, sir,' said the duke, 'your Majesty may cause the matter to be discussed secretly by your learned men, without any rumour at all.' 'Very well,' said the King, 'and so shall it be.' And thus inspired by God, he called divers of his great and trusty doctors unto him, charging them distinctly to examine what law of God should direct so carnal a man as Campeggio, under the name of spiritual, to judge a king in his own realm; according unto whose commandment these doctors resorting together into an appointed place disputed this matter *large et stricte*, as the case required. And as the black by the white is known; so, by conference of the oppositions together, it appeared that the evangelical law varied much from the canon law in this point; so that, in effect, because two contraries cannot stand *in uno subjecto eodem casu et tempore*, they were constrained to recur unto the King's Majesty's pleasure to know whether of these two laws should be preferred: who, smiling at the ignorance of so fond a question, answered, that the Gospel of Christ ought to be the absolute rule unto all others; commanding them therefore to follow the same without regard either to the civil, canon, or whatsoever other law.

'And here began the quick. For these doctors had no sooner taken the Gospel for their absolute rule but they found this Popish authority over the kings and princes of the earth to be usurped. For Peter himself, whose successor the Pope presumeth to be, commandeth all Christians, whatsoever they be, to obey and honour kings and princes with fear and reverence; because the kings of the earth are ordained of God. And so saith Paul, so saith Solomon, and so Christ himself by example hath commanded, when entering into Capernaum, he humbled himself unto the payment of the Prince's custom. And if Peter, Paul, Solomon, and Christ himself, said they, have directed us to the obedience of kings in the time when there was no Christian king in the world, how much more now ought all Christians to obey their princes absolutely; when they, the kings themselves, are not only members of the self-same body of Christ, but also members of the Christian justice? And what greater dishonour, said they, can a king receive than in his own realm to be made a subject, and to appear, not before another virtuous king or emperor, but before a vile, vicious beast grown out of the dunghill? And again, what more can be done unto a murderer or a thief than to bring him to answer in judgment? This, said they, proceedeth not of the divine law, but rather contrary, forasmuch as the spiritual office of the Christian religion proceedeth altogether by charitable counsel.

'Of their just and evangelical conclusion his Highness resolved of that he had to do; and with patience of his past error, licensed the said Cardinal Campeggio to return unto Rome, not so highly rewarded as the said cardinal looked for, nor yet with such commission as Pope Clement thought should have mended his hungry purse for the new licence that he had prepared unto the King's second marriage. For immediately after Campeggio his departure, the King, assoiled in conscience of his first divorced matrimony, both by the law of God and also by the public consent of the whole Church of England and his Barony and his Commons, proceeded unto his second marriage without further bribe or suit unto the Pope. So that Clement, seeing his line broken, and the fish escaped with the hook and bait, like a mad raging dog vomited his fulminations, and by consistorial censures excommunicated both King and country, affirming that the King began to rebel against the Roman See for none other but because his holy Fatherhood would not grant him the licence of this new marriage; and with this new leasing brought the King in slander of the ignorant and superstitious world. And here may you see how the multitude is blinded.*

'But to let you know with how much reason he hath disannulled the Papal authority, I doubt not but that every humble heart doth know, that one infinite God is He who governeth all, both heaven and earth, and that utterly. Neither the name nor the glory of God can be attributed to any creature; so that by consequence the Pope is no earthly god, as the canon laws witness him to be; and then how foolish a thing it is to believe that he hath God's power by Christ, I shall report me unto you when I have said my reason. The Pope allegeth himself Christ's Vicar, Peter's successor, and by Peter's keys to have power to loose and bind in heaven, earth, and hell. First, for Christ's Vicar, it is manifest, it is certain that in the whole Scripture there is not one word mentioned how Christ ordained any vicar or subject here in earth to be his broker or factor in matters of salvation or damnation: but the express contrary is found that Christ himself is only the Way, the Verity, and the Life, without whom none can have access unto the Father; and again, none knoweth the Father but the Son, and

---

* See Note B. page 85.

to whom the Son vouchsafeth to reveal Him; no man cometh unto the Son, but whom the Father draweth. Moreover, Christ saith that He is the gate by which all they that be saved must enter; and besides Him, there is none other foundation, nor in none other name health, saith Peter. Paul crieth out that Christ only is justification and only Mediator between God and man, and saith not between God and the Pope. So that it is impossible to prove by the Holy Scriptures the Pope to be another mediator to distribute the merits that Christ saith He will distribute Himself. For if Christ be perfect God, and God everywhere, then God in Christ doth continually work His perfection—that is to say, salvation in the faithful, and judgment on the infidels, as the Holy Scriptures undoubtedly do affirm, without any need of the Pope's help in that behalf. And if Christ were but man only, and imperfect as the Pope would make Him to be in this case where he pretendeth to be His vicar or attorney, then our faith being vain in Christ, *à fortiori* must be more than vain in the Pope. For the Pope dispenseth not earthly things, neither treasure nor health of body, as his covetous gathering of gold and self-infirmity of reason proveth; and as for celestial things, I speak of the soul, being a carnal man, though well he had the spirit of prophecy, yet could he nought judge thereof.

'Now unto that he presumeth of Peter's succession, it cannot be found in the Holy Scriptures that ever Peter came to Rome, but dwelled in Antioch, preaching there the word of God all the days of his life. So the Bishop of Antioch should of reason be rather Peter's successor than the Bishop of Rome; and the keys that were given to Peter appear not by the Gospel to be given to any successor, but to Peter only, who had no less of the Holy Ghost than the Pope hath of the devil. And what effect those keys have, it may well be seen, when we consider our own miserable sins which ye believe lieth in him to bind or to loose. If I never sin, how can he bind me? and if I sin, I bind myself. If it please God in Christ to pardon me my sins, what devil can annoy me? And if God will not forgive me, what creature can bring me unto heaven? So that, unless you will say that the Pope is greater than God, and can enforce God and Christ to make and mar as He will, you must needs confess the Pope's authority to be utterly vain and superstitious. My duty of reverence reserved towards religion, speaking by protestation, I shall tell you merely how these keys came to Peter.

'Christ having bolted the gates of heaven and barred the door on the inward side, bade Peter keep those keys safe until the day of judgment. Before that time, He would that none should corporally enter in there by the gate, but fly in spirit over the wall. So that Peter all the days of his life sought to lead all true Christians thither by lively faith, as his Master taught him, and not by opening the gates; and therefore hid the keys in his habitation at Antioch, where they lay many years, unknown. At length, in the time of Phocas, the Emperor of Constantinople, a simple priest found them, and marvelling at the curious workmanship (being, as they were, of divine operation), to gratify his Lord the Emperor with so rare a thing, went and presented them to his Majesty, who, not knowing how to use them, gave them after unto Pockyface (I would say Boniface the Third), by whom they were first brought into the Roman Church. But in effect this Boniface, seeking the gates of heaven, failed of his way, and, by misfortune, happened on the gates of hell, where, unwittingly, he put those keys in use, and in very deed, at once opened them; *quia portæ inferni non prevalebunt adversus eum;* in such wise that the devils got out and, by plain force, after they had drawn Boniface in, kept the gates so wide open, that all they who have followed Boniface in the Papistical belief, thinking to climb to heaven, are fallen there by the way.

'Finally, to conclude of this Popish authority. It was not only found that the Pope was a false prophet, a deceiver and beguiler of human souls, but also the same Antichrist whom John accuseth in so many figures of his Apocalypse, forasmuch as Antichrist can be no otherwise expounded but Christ's contrary. And the Pope is so contrary unto Christ by Daniel, that the matter was *toto* evident; for whereas Christ was humble, patient, chaste, poor, constant, and obedient, seeking always the fulfilling of His Father's will and not His own, the Pope, clean contrary, was proud, impatient, lecherous, rich, inconstant, and disobedient, not seeking the fulfilling of any part of God's will, but his own will only, in despite of all the world. As for proof, Christ humbled Himself to the washing of His apostles' feet; patiently suffered the Scribes and Pharisees to contend with Him; chastely resisted the worldly possessions of the devil's temptation in the desert; lived poorly without any habitation of His own; was constant in the fulfilling of the law, for the sins of His Father's elected; and last of all, obediently suffered death, offering Himself alone, crowned with thorns, upon the tree of the cross, for the redemption of all the number of the true Christians. And the Pope that arrogantly maketh not the mean people, but the Emperor himself, to kiss his foot, impatiently can he abide any man that would speak against his tyranny and abomination; resisteth not, but rather embraceth, the unchaste, devilish temptation—that is to wit, *omnia regna mundi;* liveth more richly in his sumptuous and imperial palaces of his own; hath no kind of constancy in doing any good thing that God's law commandeth, but hath so much to do with the merchandize of other men's sins that he cannot see to reckon with his own (for that little constancy that he hath is only in persecuting Christ's faithful); and, finally, is disobedient both unto God and nature, offering himself crowned with so many crowns of gold to the destruction of so many numbers of men, as daily be slain of all hands for his only cause. And it was not only proved that the Pope was thus contrary unto Christ in his doings, but also in his doctrine and ceremonies from the first to the last, too long now to rehearse; yea, and that not this living Pope alone, but all they that are dead, being comprehended under that name, especially from the time of the said Boniface the Third forwards. For though the Popes have been diverse in outward customs, some less wicked than others, yet in their inward hypocrisy they have all followed the devil's dam. But what need I to say so much, since I hear say there is a tragedy, entitled *Free Will*, which so well describeth his colours that there needeth no more doubt of the matter?'

'As you say,' said my Contrary, 'I have heard much reasoning of this tragedy; but the learned men condemn it, and say that it hath neither form nor fashion of a tragedy.'

'And wot you why?' said I. 'Because the tragedy condemneth the abomination of these your learned men, and therefore now that they can find no answer to deface the truth thereof, they only contend with the proportion. And are these the members of your Mother, the Holy Church?' 'Why,' said he, 'what can you say by our Mother, Holy Church?' 'I say,' quoth I, 'that she is an arrant whore, a fornicatress, and an adultress with the princes of the earth, and an express enemy of the Father, Son, and Holy Ghost, and of the lawful Church, the Espouse of Christ; for as Christ, the Son of God, in lawful matrimony engendereth on His Holy Church, by the spawn of His blood spread on the cross, all the lawful begotten children of salvation in faith and charity, so the Pope, son of the devil, your god on earth, in fornication engendereth on your whorish Mother Church all the bastards of perdition that believe remission of sin in him by ignorance and superstition.'

At the which words, my said adversary, all swelling with anger, approached me with his dagger to have stricken me; but the other gentlemen present, and in my quarrel, threatened him, assuring him that they would take my part when there should happen me any need, and so pacified him sooner than me, who, for the present fear, remembered not where I was; for his sudden fury gave occasion of many words and much ado, and long it was ere ever my spirits were quieted. Finally, my memory returned, and being required of these gentlemen to proceed unto the rest of my purpose, seeing them earnestly attentive to hear me, in manner of exclamation, thus I began to say :—

'Oh, Free Will! where art thou? Oh, Patience! oh, Humility! oh, Discretion! what have I offended you? And yet I wis I little need to marvel, since common experience yieldeth me an approved answer; for when I regard the discourse of Philosophy, all said reckoned, I find the will of man in the bosom of his appetite, notwithstanding that the wise philosophers have ever coveted to place the will between reason and the appetite, indifferently inclinable unto either part at the man's free election. But now, to prove that the appetite against reason draweth no less the will unto him than substance of the earth and water, against the air and fire, draweth the body unto the heavy centre, I will seek no other witness but this gentleman's own sudden motion against me. For you all can testify there was no man interrupted him whilst he said what he could against the honour of my Sovereign Lord the King deceased, of whom he hath used the extremest terms he could devise. And, again, I presumed not to defend him until, with one voice, you all had given me the charge and commission so to do. So that reason would he should semblably have given me quiet audience, not to speak as an indifferent, but as his plain contrary. But when his appetite, hanging heavy in the balance, had drawn his will so low that reason was clean out of sight, then wrought his choler the venom that he would have vomited against my truth. For this will I offer, that if I be proved a liar, I am content, not only to abide your sentence, but also that punishment which he himself shall judge me worthy.' With which words I paused, so that they, fearing I would say no more, began of new to assure me from hurt, and prayed me not to leave off so lightly, but to return to my enterprised matter.

'3. 'Well,' said I, 'to satisfy you, I would take on me much more labour than this, and therefore, following my reason as touching the Bishop of Rochester and Thomas More, whom the King's Majesty caused to be beheaded, if I should say that they were not learned I should impugn the verity. But in very deed their learning was much more grounded on the Thomistical, Aristotelical, and Scholastical philosophy, than in the Gospel of Christ, as hereafter you shall perceive. For when the King's Highness was fully persuaded to understand the Pope's usurped power, not by these my rehearsed authorities, but by more proofs than a whole Bible would contain, and by the consent of the greatest learned men's opinions of all the universities of Christendom, as there be divers alive in Padua, Pavia, Bologna, Paris, and elsewhere can testify, whose counsel his Majesty examined or ever he would attempt the disannulling and extirping thereof; his Highness then, I say, called his general Parliament, without which he determined no great matter. And this Parliament, to let you wit, is divided into two councils—the one of the Nobility and Prelates, and the other of the Commons of the realm; that is to say, two of the wisest men of every city, of every great borough, and of every province of his dominion. Now, amongst these councils this Popish matter was propounded, and there was *pro et contra* held and kept more than a whole year long; for in the Parliament the law permitteth all men to speak without danger, as well against as with the King. So that the old superstition having more authority in their obstinate hearts than the present verity, would not give place unto the King's purpose, until by open preaching throughout the realm, the blind people began so manifestly to see, that many of them who before most earnestly favoured the Pope became then his greatest enemies. Whereof there followed a statute, made by the same Parliament, that no man upon pain of death should call the Pope other than the Bishop of Rome, nor in any wise maintain—and thus ceased the Pope's revenue—his quarrel of Peter-pence, of jubilees, of indulgences, of pardons and dispensations, and such other baggage as beforetime availed the Pope's purpose better than 100,000 ducats a year out of England.

'You must now, nevertheless, understand that though this act passed so in the Parliament, yet all the parties in the same consented not unto it; for the judgment in the Parliament cases is given by dividing the persons; all that say yea on the one side of the House, and all that say nay on the other side, and the most number do always attain the sentence. And so the purpose of the Bishop of Rochester, and More, among the rest, held with the negative part, according to their consciences, as I suppose. For when they saw the contrary to have place then hanged they down their heads, and murmured against the King, provoking his displeasure otherwise than it became subjects to do, and his Majesty thinking nevertheless by reason and fair means and time to persuade them, supported their ignorance more than nine months. But when their predestinate mischief would not suffer his benignity to overcome their hardened hearts, and that the King at length perceived their invincible obstinacy to have a beginning of operation—for the cardinal's hat was already upon the way coming to the said Bishop of Rochester, not only as a worthy reward of his merit, but also as a buckler under the which the Pope thought to handle his cruel sword—his Highness, I say, fearing the example of his predecessor, King John, or ever the hat arrived, shaved the bishop's crown by the shoulders, to see afterwards where the Pope could bestow his cardinal's hat; and served More of the same after he had left them both four months in prison, and used all the means possible to dissuade them from their errors.'

Here one of the gentlemen asked me what was that King John that I had named. To whom I answered that he was one that being King of England more than 300 years agone, sought that time to confound the Pope's usurped authority like as the last King had done; but because his bishops had at that time more power in his own realm than he, after seven years' excommunication he was constrained to renounce his royal crown into the Pope's hands; remaining private a certain space, he at length came on his knees before the Pope's legate to be assoiled, and there thankfully received his crown again. Was he not, trow you, well entreated? I wot he was, forsooth, and finally well rewarded; for a holy monk poisoned him, and so his miserable reconcilement had a miserable end.

'4. And as for the King's usurping of the Papal authority in dispensation of the Papal ecclesiastical bishoprics and benefices, I am sure that it is not unknown to you that every secular lord, as they call them in most places of their dominions, have disposed time out of mind, and given the private benefices to what priests it hath pleased them by the authority of the name of patrons of those benefices. So that the King, having tried the substance of the Papal authority with no less diligence than alchemists do the metals at the fire, finding himself absolute patron of his private Christian dominion, thought it more meet, as Prince and Apostle, to attend himself unto the making and ordering of the bishops of the English Church, than to suffer one foreign bishop to make another by only information of the great carrier Mr. Money; and therefore enterprised to know both the person and bishopric, or ever he would dispose the golden mitre and silver pastoral.

'But in the other things he hath nothing followed the Papal dignity. For whereas the Pope, by his indulgences and jubilees, draweth the person unto idolatry to trust remission of sins in his beastly authority, and by dispensations encourageth men to commit perjury, adultery, fornication, usury, murder, and infinite other such, contrary to God's commandment, the King hath not willed to transform himself into the idol of neither of these two cases by promising pardon of sins to them that believe in him, or by dispensing with the damnable doings of the wicked, but hath willed all men to be obedient unto the laws of justice, acknowledging himself to be less than a perfect man, and not more than a godly Christian, as the Pope presumeth to be:—the trial whereof is evident by the answer of Christ himself unto the mother of the sons of Zebedee, when He said it lay not with Him to grant the sitting in heaven on His right hand or on His left unto John and James, for they must sit there whom God the Father hath ordained thereunto; and the Pope, remitting *pœna et culpa*, taketh out of heaven and thrusteth into hell, and out of hell by the way of his Purgatory carrieth into heaven whom it pleaseth him, placing this saint amongst the quire of martyrs, and that other amongst the virgins, confessors, and holy fathers, patriarchs, and false prophets, as he list to canonize them; of which canonization our St. Thomas of Canterbury is one, whose spoiled shrine and burned bones seemeth so greatly to offend your conscience.

'5. And it is true, I cannot deny, but that the King's Majesty found a wonderful great treasure about the same: for in the space of more than 250 years, I think, there have been few kings or princes of Christendom that did not either bring or send some of their richest jewels thither; and I report me unto you then, what the recourse of the common people was to see that holy sepulchre, being so preciously adorned with gold and stone, that at midnight you might in some manner have discovered all things as well as at noon day.

'But now to speak of this saint's life and holiness in few words—I shall relate unto you the effect of this story. His father was an English merchant, but his mother was a Paynim, I wot not of what part of Barbary; and he, the said saint, was brought up at school, where he studied so long that at length he became well learned in the canon laws, and then, grown unto man's years, he was brought by friendship to the Court of the King, and made the King's chaplain. This King was named Henry the Second; and in process of time began so to favour this blessed Saint Thomas for his courtly behaviour, that, by little and little, he exalted him from chaplain to a councillor, from councillor to bishop, and from bishop to the highest unto himself—that is to say, Lord Chancellor of England. Finally, this Henry the Second, by good occasion, began to perceive the error of this malignant Church that reigneth still here among you; and like a good Christian Prince, would gladly have reformed it, first, with correcting of the ministers' abominable life, and after with the due consequent remedies. But this holy saint having for his part the archbishopric of Canterbury, metropolitan of all the others, with as good as 50,000 ducats of yearly revenue, valiantly resisted him, and had that courage that, apparelled in his pontificals, with the mitre and golden cross, in the King's presence, he

accursed all of them that, in deed or word, would
offend his Holy Mother Church, or any minister of
the same; insomuch that the King, kindled by
his just disdain, banished him out of his sight, and
after remembering how villanously his unkind slave
in his own realm sought of a King to make him a
subject, sent some of his officers to lay hand on him.
But this saint, advised hereof by way of traitorous
intelligence, escaped out of the realm, and fled unto
Rome, where of the Pope he was worthily received, *quia mutuo militabant.* And hereupon the
Holy Roman Consistory excommunicated the King
and all his partakers, and openly interdicted the
realm of England, which interdiction had so much
the more effect, by as much as the other bishops
that remained at home were of more authority than
the King: so that, in term of four years there was
no mass sung, nor other like good thing said in the
churches. Finally, the Pope wrought so much
with the Most Christian King, and the Most Christian with the less Christian, that the saint was
reconciled, the priests licensed to consecrate, and
the Holy Mother Church in peace; but there was a
triumph with ringing of bells, I trow.

'Well, sir, in conclusion, this blessed Saint
Thomas would not thus be contented, but after a
certain time his choler began to work, that he
ashamed not openly to use, I wot not what oppro-
brious words against the King, which one day were
referred to his Grace as he sat at meat. 'Yea,' said
the King, 'have I brought him up of nought to
drive me out of my realm? If I were served with
men as I am with women, he should not thus con-

tend with me in mine own house.' These words were marked of them that waited at the table, in such wise that, without more ado, even four of those gentlemen waiters conferred together, and straightway took their journey to Canterbury, where, tarrying their time, one evening finding the bishop in the common cloister, after they had asked him certain questions, whereto he most arrogantly made answer, they slew him. And thus began the holiness. For incontinently as these gentlemen were departed, the monks of that monastery locked up the church doors, and persuaded the people that the bells fell on ringing by themselves; and there was crying of 'Miracles! miracles!' so earnestly, that the devilish monks, to nourish the superstition of this new-martyred saint, having the place long time separate unto themselves, *quia propter sanguinem suspenduntur sacra*, corrupted the fresh water of a well there with a certain mixture, that many times it appeared bloody, which, they persuaded, should proceed by miracle of the holy martyrdom. And this water marvellously cured all manner infirmities, insomuch that the ignorant multitude came running thither of all lands; especially after that these false miracles were confirmed by the Pope's canonization, which followed within four years after, as soon as the Roman See had ratified the saint's glory in heaven. Yea, and more; these feigned miracles had such credit at length, that the poor King himself was persuaded to believe them, and, in effect, came in person to visit the holy place, with great repentance for his passed well-doing; and for the satisfaction of his sins, gave many great and fair possessions unto the monastery of the aforesaid religious. And thus, finally, was this holy martyr sanctified of all hands. But the King's Majesty that now is dead, finding the manner of this saint's life to agree ill with proportion to a very saint, and marvelling at the virtue of this water that healed all diseases, as the blind world believed, determined to have substantial proof of this thing, and, in effect, found these miracles to be utterly false. For when the superstition was taken away from the ignorant multitude, then ceased also the virtue of this water, which now remaineth plain water, as all other waters do. So that the King, moved of necessity, could no less do than deface the shrine that was author of so much idolatry. Whether the doing thereof hath been the undoing of the canonized saint or no, I cannot tell; but this is true, that his bones are spread amongst the bones of so many dead men, that, without some great miracle, they will not be found again.'

'By my troth,' said one of the gentlemen, 'in this your King did as I would have done.'

'What?' said my adversary, 'do you credit him?'

'Within a little,' said that other; 'for his tale is sensible. And I have known of the like false miracles here in Italy proved before my face.'

'6. 'Now,' quoth I, 'hearken well unto me in this mine answer against miracles, and you shall hear things of another sort. In times past, England hath been occupied with more pilgrimages than Italy is now. For as you have here our Lady in so many places—di Loretto, di Gracia, di Miracoli, l'Annunciata, di Fiorenza, San Roches, San Antonio di Padua that presented God's body to an ass, and so many others as ye know; even so had we our Lady of Walsingham, of Penrice, of Islington, St. Thomas, St. John of Salstone that conjured the devil into a book, and so many holy roods that it was a wonder. And here and there ran all the world; yea, the King himself, till God opened his eyes, was as blind and obstinate as the rest. I mean in the time when he wrote against Martin Luther. And those roods and these our Ladies were all of another sort than these your saints be; for there were few of them but that with engines that were in them could beckon, either with their heads and hands, or move their eyes, or manage some part of their bodies, to the purpose that the friars and priests would use them; and especially one Christ Italianate, that with the head answered yea and nay at all demands.

'But, among the rest, I shall tell you one thing especially. In a certain monastery called Hailes, there was a great offering to the blood of Christ, brought thither many years agone out of the Holy Land of Jerusalem; and this blood had such virtue that, as long as the pilgrim was in deadly crime, his sight would not serve him to regard it, but incontinently as he was in the state of grace he should clearly behold it. See here the craft of these devilish soul-quellers! It behoved each person that came thither to see it, first to confess himself, and then, paying a certain to the common of the monastery, to enter into a chapel, upon the altar whereof this blood should be showed him. There, meanwhile, by a secret way behind the altar, came the monk that had confessed him, and presented upon the altar a pix of crystal, great and thick as a ball on the one side and thin as a glass on the other side; in the which the blood on the thin side was open and clear to the sight, and on the thick side impossible to be discerned. Now if this holy confessor thought by the confession that he had heard that the quality of the party confessed would yield him more money, then showed he forth the thick side of the pix, through which the blood was invisible; so that the person, seeing himself remain in deadly sin, must turn and return to his confessor, till, by paying for masses and other such alms, he had purchased the light of the thin side of the crystal, and then was he safe in the favour of God until he fell in sin again. And what blood, trow you, was this? These monks (for there were two especially and secretly appointed to this office) every Saturday killed a duck, and revived therewith this consecrated blood, as they themselves confessed, not only in secret but also openly, and before an approved audience.

'And was this miracle, think you, alone? No, no, alas! if I should train you with the rehearsal of spiritual miracles, I should tell you of thousands as true as this, or rather better; for we had holy maidens that lived not by manna as the Jews in the desert, but by food of impalpable spirits; and such as could tell all the secrets of God, and how all men's matters went in heaven; whereunto this your gallant auricular confession was so diligent a minister that it were a wonder to tell. And can you blame the King though he hanged and burned those hypocritical knaves and whores that were authors and actors of so much abomination and superstition? And did he not as good service unto God in destroying the places of these imaginary saints that drew the people unto the belief and trust of these false miracles, as the good Hezekiah, King of Judah, did in destroying the Mosaical brazen serpent and overthrowing the excelsa, the images, and hallowed woods consecrated to their idols? Yea, undoubtedly did he. For all the miracles that the blind people conceive to proceed from these images, or by means of these represented saints, are clean repugnant to the Christian faith, and also unto God's perfection. And the reason is this: God is only divine and perfect, who by His Divinity of nought hath created all things, and in His perfection containeth and governeth all things to that end that He immutably hath determined. And every angel, every devil, and every man is a creature without either deity or perfection, since everything that hath beginning or end is imperfect. And whereas God is present everywhere, and worketh all in all things as Paul affirmeth, the creature, contrarily, is present only to the place of his service; as the angels in heaven, the devils in hell, and the men in earth. Now to my purpose; if the saints, who are creatures, be in heaven, and want, as they do indeed, the perfection of God's Divinity, how is it possible that, absent from the earth, the saints, whom the earthly man imagineth for his advocates, should hear the man's prayer, though well he would cry with a trumpet's voice towards heaven, *Sancta Maria, ora pro me?* And again, none knoweth man's thoughts but God alone; neither angel, saint, nor devil; for the Scriptures affirm God to be the only Searcher of the heart; so that, neither hearing me nor knowing my heart, it is impossible how the saints should be means of my relief. And as it is proved before, the Holy Scriptures affirm Christ to be only Mediator betwixt God and man, prohibiting all faithful Christians to seek other means; for who recurreth to the saint cannot deny but that he trusteth sooner to speed that way than by the immediate going unto Christ, and so doubteth in Him in whom only he ought to trust. For maintenance of which their infidelity these sophistical theologians have made them a god of glass, wherein they imagine the saints to behold our necessities, appointing every one of them unto a private office; like as first one Dennis, and after him Thomas of Aquinas, hath placed the offices of angels, this to the cherubim and that to the flying seraphim, that other to the dominations, and so forth, after his own fantastical imagination, contrary to the doctrine of Paul, who, being ravished to the third heavens, saw things not lawful to be spoken: whereas this blessed Thomas, ravished in his own conceit above all the heavens, hath spoken of the celestial spirits things that he never heard nor saw. But the ignorant multitude that are always more inclinable unto error than unto the truth, have tasted such a savour in their imaginations, that because God commonly granteth not the things that they most desire, they therefore have framed gods that will do for them when they be prayed unto, believing the better to attain their purpose by many than by one.

'And hereof hath it followed that when some person hath escaped any imminent danger, recovered health from a grievous sickness, or cure of a sore wound, passed some dangerous tempests of the sea, or obtained some victory in arms, or some riches or possessions, incontinently he yieldeth thanks therefore unto his familiar advocate in heaven, by whose means he imagineth to have received such benefits; which otherwise the mutable God, as he believeth, would never have granted him; and therefore runneth to this or that image with candles, torches, lamps, incense, bells, and a thousand other tricks; affirming this and that miracle, which in effect are no other but their false and ignorant imaginations. And as to the burning of lights before those images, it is so foolish a thing that meseemeth it rather meriteth to be laughed at than spoken against. But this take I to be the reason that moveth them thereunto; because the light of the sun sufficeth not to direct the eyes of those their dumb idols by the day, therefore in the daytime do they serve them with enforced light that should serve for the night; or else they do it to blemish withal the brightness of the sun, whose light may perchance be no less enemy to their nature than contrary to the light of the night owl; for by right they agree so well with the dark, that till the sun's arising, they need no light at all. This I speak for the formal saints; for that deformed body, which, of all others, is supposed to have most life, may in no wise want light in the night, but perchance he should happen to arise at some inconvenient hour. But what need I thus to occupy myself with those foolish saints and pilgrims, since the thing is now so manifest unto all men that have eyes, that who is he that cannot with reason, beside the authority of the Scriptures, confound this ignorance? Wherefore I will now despite me to speak of the monasteries which his Majesty suppressed, to the intent that you may understand what was the first occasion thereof.

'7. And thus. When his Highness had found out the falsehood of these jugglers, who led the people unto this idolatry of worshipping of saints, believing of miracles, and going on pilgrimage here and there (as unto this hour you see it used here in Italy), being persuaded by the presumption of these special things that I have rehearsed, and of infinite others too long now to be mentioned, that these abominable friars were the very false prophets and roaring wolves whom Christ prophesieth in the Gospel should come under the apparel of lambs to devour the flock of true Christians—his Majesty, for the better discovering of these hypocrites, sent forth commissioners into all the provinces of his realm, to examine particularly the manner of living that these ribalds used. Now came the matter fully to light; for when the commissioners had taken upon them the charge of this examination, and began one by one to examine these friars, monks, and nuns upon their oaths, sworn upon the Evangelists, there were discovered hypocrisies, murders, idolatries, miracles, sodomies, adulteries, fornications, pride, and not 7, but more than 700,000 deadly sins.

'Alas! my heart maketh all my members to tremble with another manner of fever than is the quartain, when I remember all the abomination that there was tried out. Oh Lord God (speaking under correction), what canst Thou answer to the Five Cities consumed with celestial fire, when they shall allege before Thee the iniquities of those religious whom Thou hast so long supported? Note well (said I), these few words, and I shall tell you:—In their dark and sharp prisons there were found dead so many of their brethren that it was a wonder; some crucified with more torments than ever men heard of, and some famished only for breaking of their superstitious silence, or some like trifle; and especially on some children there was used a cruelty not to be spoken with human tongue. There was of the hermits some one that, under colour of confession, had used carnally with more than 200 or 300 gentlewomen and women of reputation, whose names, enrolled by commandment, they showed unto the commissioners, insomuch that some of the selfsame commissioners found of their own wives titled among the rest, with what conscience I report me unto you. There was working of wonders; the friars and nuns were as whores and thieves in the open street, and there were saints that made the barren women bring forth children; unto whom there wanted no resort from all parts of the kingdom. Alas! what should I say when Ptolemy his discourse, Pliny his memory, and Augustine his pen, joined in one man, should not satisfy to make him an apt author of so detestable a history as this abomination requireth?

'Well, to my purpose. In conclusion, upon the return of these commissioners, when the King was fully informed of the case, incontinently he called his Parliament; but, or ever the councillors of the same could assemble together, here came that abbot, and there came that prior; now came that abbess, and there came that prioress from all parts of the realm unto the King, offering their monasteries into his hands; beseeching him to pardon them their sins *de pœnâ* only, and not *de culpâ;* insomuch that his Majesty accepted many of them, and pardoned them all except a few only of the most notable ribalds, whom, for the others' example, he caused to suffer death in divers ways as their horrible cases diversely merited. And thereupon following the said Parliament, in the which all these matters were not only published, but also confessed by the false religious persons brought openly in judgment, it was concluded, both by the Barons and also by the Commons of the said Parliament, that these monasteries should be extirped, and the goods and revenues thereof disposed as the King and his council should think it expedient. He had made his learned doctors to search out the grounds of these many evils of religion, who, conferring the same substantially with the Gospel, found it to be clean contrary to the Christian religion, by many more reasons than I can well remember. Nevertheless, for your satisfaction, I shall here rehearse one or two of them, to the intent you may the better taste what wickedness that superstitious religion doth comprehend.

'First, the religious do profess themselves to live much more nobly than the secular people do, and by as much as they can, will persuade the world that they are no sinners, but just and upright persons, by which reason they have wiped themselves clean out of Christ's vocation, who saith He came not to call the just person but the sinner. And then the good works that they pretended to do are all outward works; as apparelling themselves in religious habits, singing and roaring in the quire, saying of their service in Latin, with matins and masses, and holy abstinence from flesh this day and that morrow, when they have filled their bellies with good fish, fruit, and wine. And such other are their holy outward operations; whereas Christ exhorteth us to beware that we work not our justice before man, but secretly in giving of alms, that the one hand know not what the other doth; in quiet and hearty prayers; in fastings, and charity, and so forth; of which inward virtues those religious are known to be utterly void.

'Furthermore, the vows that these religious make, and that they teach others to make, are clean repugnant to Christ's doctrine, who teacheth His faithful evermore humbly to submit themselves to the will of the Father, as by the example of His prayer which He made in the garden the night before His death, it is manifest. For when the flesh had prayed the Father to deliver Him from that present passion, incontinent the spirit rebuked Himself, saying, 'No, Father; not as I will, but as Thou wilt.' And yet these religious promising unto God that which already they are bound to observe—that is to say, chastity, charity, obedience, and poverty, which in effect the infirmity of the flesh alloweth no creature to perform—will not that God deal with them as He will, but as they will themselves; who with their superstitious works will enforce God to give them, not only health and wealth in this world, but also Paradise in the other world; and by their example have taught the ignorant multitude not to content themselves with the infirmities, adversities, poverties, persecutions, and passions that God sendeth them in this world, but with vows of images, of tables, of pilgrimage, of change of apparel, and of such other baggage, to enforce God by His saints, and not by Christ, to give them health, prosperity, riches, and joy, according to their inconstant pleasure. And hereof hath followed the building of monasteries, synagogues, chapels, chantries, with burning of lights, incense, singing of masses, and ringing of bells, when the blind people have believed with these worldly trifles to gratify the Divine Majesty. But what saith the prophet? what saith Stephen? what saith Paul? 'God,' say they, 'dwelleth not in temples made with hands, nor can receive nothing of any earthly matter; for what things have we here that He hath not created, and what availeth it unto God our foolish sacrifices?' As David saith, 'If thou, Lord, wouldst have sacrifices, I would have offered them unto Thee, but the incense pleaseth Thee not.' The true sacrifice, therefore, unto God, is the humble, contrite, and contented spirit, and not these temples, incenses, images, flesh, fish, or fruit. And so much found those doctors to say against those religious that, in conclusion, they condemned them to be worse infidels and enemies unto God than the idolater Caffraries of India found out by the Portugals.'

'Caffraries,' said one of the gentlemen, 'what be they, I pray you?'

'They be,' said I, 'a certain people that do worship the devil in images, as you do here the saints.'

'And by what reason,' said he, 'should they worship the devil?'

'By such a reason,' said I, 'as will make you to wonder. First, they believe one virtuous God to be the universal Creator of all things, who, in His perfection, must needs be just. And then, by the only law of nature, and by the malice that reigneth in the flesh, they acknowledge themselves in envy and other such to be contrary unto the divine virtue, so that the justice, as they believe, cannot less do than condemn them unto perpetual damnation, whereof the devil is minister; and so imagining that who most devoutly serveth the devil in this world, must of reason receive of him most favour when he cometh to him in the other world, they therefore most diligently observe infinitely their ceremonies unto the devil with fasting, alms, and prayer, in hope that their present penance shall be a mitigation of their pains to come. Tell me now, I pray you, how you like all this.'

'As I do all the rest,' said my Contrary; 'for in this case you prefer them that serve the devil before the servants of God.'

'No,' said I, 'you mistake me. For your monks, friars, and nuns, I say, serve not God, but serve themselves, proudly presuming against God to be just, holy, and righteous of themselves; whereas the other poor idolaters confessed God only to be virtuous and themselves to be sinners; and therefore will I so prefer them, that if they had knowledge of God's mercy in Christ as we have, I fear me their works would prove much more Christian than ours do. But come we to an end with these our religious. Finally, these doctors found that Paul in his Epistles had reproved the Christians for dividing themselves after the manner of these Christian preachers, who had been ministers unto their conversion, because some one said, 'I am of Paul;' and another said, 'I am of Apollos;' 'I of Cephas;' and 'I of Christ.' What said Paul? 'Was I crucified for you? Is Christ divided among you? No,' said he, 'I have taught you to be one self thing in Christ in those divisions, either of name or of doing.' So that, in conclusion, these orders of Francis and Dominick, of Bennet and Bridget, and of so many others, were condemned by those doctors as things clean contrary unto the true Christian religion, in which all the faithful to Christ bound in one knot of charity, in belief of clean remission of sins, are regenerate to one self order and rule, without difference either of name, habit, order, or colour. Wherefore, the King being clearly persuaded of all hands that this unhappy, idle, and devilish generation was to be rooted out of the world, proceeded then to the destruction of these synagogues with the self-same diligence Titus and

Vespasian used towards the destruction of Jerusalem. And did he not there as he should do, trow ye?'

'Yea,' said one of these gentlemen; 'if he had disposed these things to the use of the poor and needful, and not taken it into his own private commodity.'

'Against the poor,' said I, 'I will not speak; but thus much I will say, that if all the substance had been converted to the poor, the poor should have become richer than the princes and nobles; for our religious in England were *quasi nihil habentes et omnia possidentes*, not in spirit but in deed. I wot how your friars here in Italy observe their sworn poverty; and yet this is well true that his Majesty in divers provinces of the realm hath converted divers of these monasteries towards the bringing up of orphans and instruction of the poor, though will that part be but a small quantity in respect of the whole.

'8. And thus because I will not be tedious, having said enough, as meseemeth, unto this point, I will now answer unto the insurrection of the North,* which was cause of the death of those noblemen that my Contrary hath here spoken of.

'True it is that when those commissioners who had the charge of inquisitions on these friary matters had passed throughout the realm, here and there whereas their commissions led them, these our holy spiritual religious, who had been shriven of the lay persons with another manner of auri-

---

* See Note C. p. 104.

cular confessions than the Lently penitential sacrament requireth, suspecting the sequel of that which justly followed indeed, began with sowing of seditions here and there, to corrupt the minds of the ignorant and inconstant people; insomuch that a cobbler (mark these beginnings), encouraged by the presumptuous audacity of one private monk in the city of Lincoln, gathered unto him certain other artisans and villains such as he was himself, and in less than three days made himself a head of better than 3000 men, and under the name of Captain Cobbler, began a brave rebellion, laying hands on divers of the King's ministers, and putting some of them unto death, with robbing and spoiling some others, as it seemed them to make for their purpose, so that, had not there been gentlemen who, by fair means, by authority and friendship, pacified the ignorant multitude, no doubt of it, there should have followed such effusion of blood, such robberies and flames, as an hundred thousand flattering friars, with their catalogic sermons, could never have recompensed. Behold here the peril of this nation, who, for a cobbler and a knavish friar, not knowing any cause why, and without either money or provisions, would thus suddenly dispose themselves to war against their own blood! What, trow you, would they have done under some nobleman, upon some ground, with men and money? No, no, I shall tell you more; if this cobbler had had the knowledge how to govern these men when he had them together, to have gone forwards towards some enterprise, within less than two days more he should have found better than 20,000 men more to have followed him. But when they were together, they wist not what to do, and therefore the authority and the wisdom of the gentlemen the King's friends, without force or stripes, so confounded them, that they fled every man to his own home with more diligence than they came forth; and so the matter quieted, and a few of the principalest taken and hanged, the number was pardoned without more ado.

'But see what mischief followed of this possibility. Those our religious men knowing right well what this Captain Cobbler would have done, and not regarding what became of him indeed, disposed themselves anew to prove their fortune, being assured that if the King's Majesty should continue, there was none other but rack with them: and therefore, in the furthest part of the North, began another rebellion, the captain whereof was named Aske, a man of mean degree. And this second rebellion was of another sort than the first; for in few days they had made an army of 16 or 17,000 men, whereof there were certain noble persons, and many men of reputation, especially of the prelates of your Mother Church, for whose whorish defence all this sedition was moved. And this army came on, journey by journey, towards the heart of the realm, little less than 100 miles, until, by force of floody waters, and not by resistance of men, they were stayed before Doncaster, in the county of York. And mark here the judgment and providence of God; the King was then at Windsor Castle, besides London, making of men and putting of order here and there for his defence, as the case required; but his people came so slowly unto him, his secret superstitious enemies within his realm were so many, and the fury and power of this new-raised army so great and sudden, that he wist not well whom to trust, nor what to do; so that for extreme remedy, he sent his chief councillors unto Doncaster to treat with the rebels, to hear what they would demand, and to promise them what they would ask: which councillors used all diligence to arrive at the appointed place, where they treated with these adversaries according to their commissions. But had it not been that the waters letted them so long of their passage that their victuals and money were clean consumed, those rebels had, for that time, given small audience to any treaty. Finally, the presence of those councillors had so much authority amongst the enemies, that, with reason and fair promises, they were appeased. For when they came to reasoning, in very deed they wist not well what to demand, except the preservation of their Holy Mother Church, which their prelates and religious did evermore beat into their heads; and so, in effect, the King at that time pardoned them all, as you have alleged. Now, here cometh the matter that offendeth you. Divers of those persons, as well nobles as others, when they were returned to their quiet houses, and saw plainly that the King did constantly follow the reformation of the abominable Church, could not for all this be contented to see the things pass against their superstitious belief, but incontinently renewed the old practice of rebelling again; and in one place there were gathered together 200, in another place

100, here 50, there 20, and there 10, so that all the country was in a new rumour. But the garrisons of men that the King had this meanwhile spread through those countries, incontinently overcame those small commotions, in such wise that for fear each man withdrew him to his house. And the matter after substantially examined, the principalest of them were taken, and certain of them hanged and beheaded; that is to say, the Captain Aske, the Lord Darcy a baron, four or five knights of account, and eight or nine gentlemen, besides certain religious monks that were the ticklers of all this mischief. So that they who were put to death suffered not for their first rebellion—*that* they were pardoned for—but for the second commotion, wherein was found a continuance of their prepensed malice, not so much (as I believe) against the King's person, as against the light of the verity which their superstitious consciences would not allow. And how say you now? Know you any Prince that would have done less than this in so important a case?'

'I cannot tell you,' said mine adversary, 'how well here is manifest effusion of Christian blood.'

' Alas!' said I, ' can that hardened heart of yours relent unto no reason? Tell me, I pray you, but your opinion in this one question I shall ask you. When this body is burdened with an extreme fever, or other sickness, through the corruption of corrupt blood, the continuance whereof should put him in danger of his life, doth the physician well, by incisions of his veins, to draw away his blood that is enemy of this man's health, or were it better, by suffering it to continue, he should let the man abide in peril of destruction of his body?'

'Oh,' said my Contrary, 'what a question is this!'

'Why then,' said I, 'you must needs grant me that better it was to draw blood of a few persons who were the corruption of a whole realm, than to suffer the whole realm to perish. For if they might have had their wills, the least thing that could have followed must needs have been the bloodshedding of a stricken civil battle; and when well they had overcome the King, there would have followed none other but perpetual contention, undoing of themselves and of their neighbours, to bring their country a prey unto strange nations. But unto you there helpeth neither reason nor arguments; and therefore, since I see I cannot satisfy you, I will dispose to satisfy these gentlemen as near as I can.

'9. Now, as touching the King's so many wives, whom he chopped and changed at his pleasure (as you say), the truth is, that he hath had a great many wives, and with some of them hath had as ill-luck as any other poor man; and I shall plainly tell you, from one to one, how the matters have passed. That gentle and virtuous Lady Katherine, his first wife, was divorced from him, as you have heard, because she had been wife unto his elder brother; and in effect, within two or three years after that the King was married anew, whether it were by consumption of thought, or by course of nature, I cannot tell, she yielded her spirit unto God, leaving none other fruit behind her but her daughter, that courteous Lady Mary, whom we have so often mentioned. Now, incontinently after that divorce, the King married his second wife, as I have said, named the Lady Anne Bolene, whose liberal life were too shameful to rehearse.* Once she was as wise a woman, indued with as many outward good qualities in playing on instruments, singing, and such other courtly graces, as few women were of her time; with such a certain outward profession of gravity as was to be marvelled at. But inwardly she was all another dame than she seemed to be; for in satisfying of her carnal appetite, she fled not so much as the company of her own natural brother, besides the company of some three or four others of the gallantest gentlemen that were about the King's proper person, who were all so familiarly drawn into her train by her own devilish devices, that it should seem she was always well occupied: the busy doing whereof gave the King great cause of suspicion; so that finding by scarch the imagined mischief to have effect, he was forced to proceed therein by way of open justice, where the matter was manifested unto the whole world, and the sentence given against them: insomuch that both she and her brother, and the four other gentlemen, were beheaded: for adultery in a King's wife weigheth no less than the wrong reign of a bastard prince, which thing for a commonwealth ought specially to be regarded. And, besides this, it was laid to her charge, that she, with some of the rest, had conspired the King's death, to avoid the danger of the wickedness which they

---

* See Note D. p. 116.

perceived could not long be kept secret. And this second wife lived with the King about the space of four years, having issue a daughter by him named the Lady Elizabeth, which is at this present, at the age of fourteen years or thereabouts, a very witty and gentle young lady.

'Now when the first wife was dead and the second beheaded, then was the King undoubtedly clear of all sides; and in that estate took to wife the Lady Jane Seymour, one of the humblest and chastest maidens in the world, replete of all beauty and wisdom; who, living in perfect and loving matrimony with his Majesty the term of eighteen months or thereabouts, brought into the world that happy Prince Edward that now succeedeth the father unto the crown, in whose birth she died; a death surely much lamented of all the King's subjects, as few the like, for a woman, hath ever been heard of.*

'But to be brief. After her death the King remained a widower almost two years, till at length, upon agreement, he coupled with the sister of the Duke of Cleves, with whom he continued half a year, until information was brought him that she, the Lady Anne of Cleves, had been troth plight before with the Duke of Lorraine his son. And this report went sore unto the King's heart, who loved this woman out of measure; for why? her personage, her beauty, and gesture did no less merit it. But when he understood that she was indeed another man's wife, what for his own conscience, and what for respect of the inconvenience that in this

---

* See Note E. page 117.

case might follow unto his succession, he called his Parliament, where, after long reasoning and proof, concluding that the promise made between man and woman is it that maketh the marriage between husband and wife, and not the ceremony of the temple, his Majesty was there openly divorced from her. Howbeit, for the singular love he bare unto her, he offered her liberty to remain in England at his honourable provision, or to return into her country with worthy reward. So that she, electing England's provision, was appointed by his Majesty unto four excellent fair palaces, with all kinds of commodities, and better than 20,000 crowns of yearly revenue; wherein she liveth like a Princess as she is.*

'And thus separated from her, he married his fifth wife, named Katherine, of the house of Norfolk,† a very beautiful gentlewoman, and, to worldly judgment, a very virtuous and chaste creature, though in effect the contrary was found afterwards. For ere ever she continued two years the King's wife, it was heard that before her marriage she had contaminated her virginity, and afterwards committed, or, at the leastwise, sought means to commit, adultery. So that, in conclusion, she and two other gentlemen with her, after condemnation before the justice, were beheaded. And finally, this his last wife, likewise named Katherine, was married unto him a widow, after that she had been wife unto two noble barons of the realm, deceased. And it is thought that his Majesty married more for the

---

* See Note F. p. 121. † See Note G. p. 158.

same proof of her constant virtue than for any
carnal desire. For, remembering the dishonour
that he had received by the lightness of his other
two wives beheaded, he thought now good to fasten
upon an approved dame, as he did indeed: for this
lady hath lived thirty-three or thirty-four years without spot of blame, how well she is right fair and excellent, proportionable of body, beloved of all creatures,
and courteous as may be, whose fortune hath had
place to see the death of that husband that had
seen the death of so many wives. And, amongst all
the happy successes that the said King hath had in
this life, I reckon this one of the special, that, after
so many changes, his glorious chance hath brought
him to die in the arms of so faithful a spouse.'

'The discourse of these wives,' said one of the
gentlemen, 'is a wonderful history. But one thing
maketh me to marvel,' said he, 'that when those
wives had so offended the King, he did not rather
rid them by some fair means out of the way secretly,
than so openly to manifest his own dishonour to
the world.'

'I shall tell you why,' said I. 'In such things
his Majesty had as upright a conscience as any living
man; and, I dare say, would not have consented
unto the murder of one of them secretly for all the
goods of the world. And, again, he esteemed not
the dishonour of the matter, since the fault proceeded from the woman, who for the same suffered
open punishment; so that he accounted himself
always clear before God and man. And thus hath
he had six wives, whereof two have died in their
beds, two have suffered for adultery, and two are yet

living (as you say). But the one of them, you must consider, was the first wife before God of the Duke of Lorraine's son, as I have said before, and not unto the King. *So that he that would learn the truth of matters must covet to know as well the contra as the pro,* or ever he can judge well. For he that giveth credit unto the first information without hearing the answer, is most commonly deceived: and so were you, master mine,' said I to my Contrary.

'Good faith,' said he, ' I cannot tell what I should say; for the reports that I have rehearsed I have heard them of credible persons and of men of good intelligence, who persuaded me undoubtedly to believe as I have said. And though I have now well heard your answer, yet am I not fully persuaded; for methinketh you have set many things forth to the largest: whether they be true or not, God knoweth, for they pass my capacity.'

'At the largest!' said I; 'that is true, for I speak without respect. But here you may see what difference there is between knowledge and hearingsay. Because I know indeed, therefore I am sure of it that I speak; and because you know none otherwise but by report, therefore are you from your surety come now to doubt of your truth. Wherefore I pray God, if it be His will, so to open your heart that you be not among the number of them to whom God giveth eyes without sight and ears without hearing, to the end they should not understand the remedy of His grace.'

'As for that,' said he, 'let God do with me as Him pleaseth. But I promise you of one thing;

I would it had cost me forty crowns on the condition I had been twenty miles hence this night.'

'Why?' said I.

'Because,' said he, 'before this reasoning I was as constant a Catholic man as any was living, and now that I have heard these many arguments, I am brought into a labyrinth that I know not what way to get me out.'

'A Catholic man!' said I; 'nay, God grant you are not worse than a Jew; for whereas the Jew trusteth in his own good works and ceremonies, and nevertheless believeth in the true divine God alone, you not only trusted in your own good works (as you call them), and in the foolish ceremonies of your stepmother Church, but also have made you an earthly god of the Pope, in whose pardons you trusted more than in Christ's death. But this pleaseth me that you are come to your doubt, for so behoveth it him that out of an error will be persuaded to know the truth.

'10. And therefore, returning unto my matter, now will I answer unto the persecution of Cardinal Pole, and unto the death of his mother and friends; which, in effect, is nothing so marvellous nor so cruel as it is made here in Italy; and so I doubt not you shall well confess by that time you have heard how the things have passed. I cannot deny but that this Cardinal Pole, in very deed, is both virtuous and learned as you have commended him; for, by all men's reports that knew him, I have heard such laud and praise of his continent, patient, and charitable life, and of his great and profound doctrine, that against his person will I say nothing; but against his being this will I say, that it had been better he had died in his cradle than lived to be an occasion of so much mischief as hath followed for his sake, and is yet likely to follow.'

'Beware!' said my Contrary; 'speak not ill of him, for here be of his friends that will not hear him slandered.'

'As for my part,' said I, 'I am not his particular foe. But you must consider that I now defend not only a King's honour, but also the quiet of a whole realm, against such lewd and false reports as are sufficient to corrupt a whole world of good consciences, and to move sedition between brother and brother. So that, because the defence of this case enforceth me somewhat to touch the quick, I shall pray you to pardon me if I happen to offend you, assuring you I will for your sake forget some things that should be too homely to be spoken.

'In the time that the King's Majesty extirped and disannulled the Bishop of Rome's usurped power, as heretofore I have rehearsed, this Reginald Pole that now is cardinal, practised here in Italy, sometimes studied in the University of Padua, and sometimes in Venice, bearing the port of a gentleman, as the nobility of his house required, and was from time to time well advertised out of England of all the occurrents there; so that the law of the Parliament against the Papists was right well known unto him. Now, sir, being in Venice, the great Contarine (who of late days was by the Pope's means poisoned in Bologna for subscribing the article of Justification unto the Almaines), before his vocation unto the cardinalate, fell into such a wonderful amity and knot of friendship with this our Pole, that the one of them was never well without the other. And here began this mischief. For Contarine was no sooner crowned with the red hat but that unfortunately he sued unto the Pope to bring Pole unto the same degree; so that with much ado the Pope consented, and thus was our Pole placed in the Holy Consistory. Whether it were the earnest love of Contarine's company that blinded him, or the obstinate superstition of the Papal dignity that persuaded him, or else the ambition of the carnal glory that allured him, or what other devil moved him I cannot tell: but once no man knew better than he that the uniting of himself unto the whorish Church of Rome should bring himself and all his friends out of the King's favour, out of the good will of his country, and in perpetual excommunication of the Church of England. And what true man towards his Prince or country, if he were not mad, would then have entered into such a fury, seeing the example of the Bishop of Rochester and More, with the present estate of the realm before his face, unless he thought with the Papal power to overcome the kingly puissance? Alas! sufficed it not for a younger brother, as he is, to have an honourable entertainment at home amongst his kin and friends, where his virtue and learning might have found to have done great and high service, not only unto his Prince and King, but also unto his whole native country, the contrary whereof hath been the undoing of him and all his blood?'

'Of himself,' said my Contrary, 'that is not so;

for he liveth as honourably and in as good reputation as any other cardinal, whatsoever he be.'

'And if he were an emperor,' said I, 'being erring to his country, as he is, I can reckon him no better than most unhappy. For, if the proverb be true, 'Sweet is the love of his country,' by consequence, *the hate of his country* must needs be sour. But to my purpose. This, our Pole, had not the red hat warm on his head, but the Pope sent him in post, now to the French King, now into Spain to the Emperor, now into Flanders, now here, now there, to solicit the wars against his own native country and his Sovereign Lord and King, offering himself always to be a minister of that effect. And not contented with these outward provocations, he also wrote secretly to his mother and eldest brother to work sedition at home; and some of his letters had so ignorant *recapito* that they came to the King's hand; who, moved not only thereby, but also by many other sensible presumptions, to examine the matter, at length found out the truth, more by miracle than by human discourse. For he having retained the cardinal's youngest brother, named Sir Geoffrey Pole, only upon mistrust, without any approved matter to lay unto his charge, he in the prison desperately would have mischieved himself, which by the diligence of his ready keeper, was defended. And so being straitly examined whereupon he could have attempted so wicked an act, at last he confessed all the whole conspiracy for the which his mother and brother and those other nobles suffered, which also, or ever the year passed, was by divers other ways discovered in the proof of more effects than you would believe. For the holy religious abbots of Reading and Glastonbury had conjured the said cardinal's elder brother, named the Marquis Montague, with the other Marquis of Exeter;* and so far was the matter gone from hand to hand, that some of the King's most familiar friends, and of his Majesty's privy chamber, and of his council, were corrupted with that malicious person. Yea, and moreover, it passed conspiracy to come to effect. For part of these rebels, to the number of 800, in the second insurrection in the North, were paid with money sent them from those abbots out of the South. How say you now? Was it time, trow you, for the King to look about him?'

'These be things,' said my Contrary, 'that I never heard of.'

'No,' said I, 'there blow so many winds between the Alps and the ocean sea, that the true air of England can never arrive here into Italy uncorrupted.'

'Oh,' said he, 'and well remembered; tell me, I pray you, next unto the King's children, ought not the crown to have come unto Cardinal Pole?'

'And why unto Cardinal Pole?' quoth I.

'Because he is of the King's blood,' quoth he.

'It is true,' said I, 'he is descended of a King's blood, but it is so long ago that he is further off from this King then living, than the living Justinians of Venice are from the ancient Emperor Justinian, and as near is he to the crown as they to the empire.'

---

* See Note H. p. 162.

'Oh Lord,' said he, 'how this gear joineth with the fame of Italy.'

'And thus may you see,' said I, 'how ignorance and error reigneth amongst the multitude; and were it not for your sakes, I could tell you how the cardinal secretly professeth to be a Protestant, and openly maintaineth the Papacy with a little more hypocrisy yet than that cometh to.

'11. But I will for this time forget him, because of his new election unto the legation of England, and will speak of Ireland and Scotland, which you say the King wrongfully enforced. You must understand that the Kings of England have had dominion over a great part of Ireland these 300 years* and more, by reason whereof both the country and nation hath been divided into two sundry parts—that is to say, the English pale and the wild Irish; and like as they of the English pale always used the self-same religion, customs, laws, and manners of civil living that we use in England, so contrariwise they of the wild Irish, as unreasonable beasts, lived without any knowledge of God or good manners, in common of their goods, cattle, women, children, and every other thing, in such wise that almost there was no father which knew his son, nor no daughter that knew her father, nor yet any justice executed for murder, robbery, or any other like mischief; but the more force had ever the more reason. And hereof it followed that because their savage and idle life could not be satisfied with the only fruit of the natural unlaboured earth, there-

---

* See Note I. p. 169.

fore continually they invaded the fertile possessions of their Irish neighbours that inhabited the said English pale, reaping and mowing the corn that they sowed not, and carrying away the cattle that they nourished not. And this beastly fury which so long had reigned in this Irish nation, hath many times moved the King's predecessors with all their forces, and with great and puissant armies, to seek their destruction; but like as one poor fox in a thicket maketh the hunter with twenty couple of hounds to travail sometimes a whole day, and at length to lose his labour; so these wild Irish made those Kings, with their huge numbers of men, to beat so long the wild woods and marshes, that at length they were fain to recoil with the only gain of famine and weariness. And therefore the King's Majesty that now is dead wrought another way with them; for he layed in such substantial garrisons in the straits of his borders, that they could no more enter unto the English pale, unless they would either be slain or taken prisoners; so that, being prevented of their accustomed liberty to rob and spoil, necessity constrained them to humble themselves not only to a perpetual peace, but also to a quiet obedience and order. Yea, and when his Majesty, by policy and by the good diligence of his faithful deputy there, Sir Anthony Sillinger, had thus overcome them, to confirm his force with mercy, he rewarded divers of those wild men with great sums of his own money, appointing them places of civil honour, as earls, barons, knights, esquires, and such other as the quality of those persons seemed unto him most convenient. And by this means hath brought the nation from rude, beastly, ignorant, cruel, and unruly infidels, to the state of civil, reasonable, patient, humble, and well-governed Christians; not for desire of dominion or for avarice of revenue, but for God's honour and for a Christian peace, at his Majesty's own cost and charge, in the expense of so many thousand crowns as were too long now to tell. And look how the wild Irish before time warred against the same, even so have the Scots ever done, and yet do, against the Englishmen, like for like; by paragon, I say, in the wars only; for in their living the Scots observe a certain order both of religion and customs, though well it be somewhat barbarous. But if God had given the King his life but one or two years longer, you should surely have seen the same success of Scotland that you have heard me rehearse of Ireland; for his Majesty was resolved, either by force or by love, to have gotten in his hands that young daughter that now is heir to the Scottish crown, and by marriage of her to his son Edward, that now is our King, to have made of one self-divided nation a realm, one self perpetual united people, and peace; not for the wealth of the Scottish dominion (which, in respect of England, is of as good comparison as the barren mountains of Savoy unto the beauty of the pleasant Tuscany), but for the uniform quiet of their approved ancient contention. In very deed, if his Majesty in this case had followed the example of Joshua, to have brought his people of the desert into the champaign, I would never have gone about to excuse him; but since, contrariwise, his travail hath been to bring his people out of the champaign into the desert, which is a manifest witness against his defamed avarice, meseemeth that they are much to blame that therefore would burden him with tyranny.

'12. And as for his conscience in the motion of war against France, I would give the Emperor place to answer, whose unfortunate persuasions were occasion thereof. And what know I of the practices between the Duke and the French King? But as for the usurping of Boulogne, I say that not the Boulognaise alone but the most part of all Picardy is not sufficient to satisfy the debts that the French King did owe unto our King's Majesty; what for the money lent him to pay his ransom withal unto the Emperor when his sons lay therefore prisoners in Spain; what for the restitution of Terouenne and Tournay, which our King's Majesty conquered upon the French King in his youth; what for the tribute, and what for one thing and what for another, that it were a marvel to reckon the infinite sums of money in credit between them.'

'Tribute!' saith one of them. 'Why? doth the French King pay tribute to England?'

'Yea, that he doth,' saith I.

'And wherefore, I pray you?' quoth he.

'I shall tell you,' said I. 'More than 200 years past, when the right line of the King of France failed of heirs male, then was Isabel, the only daughter and heir of France, wife unto Edward the Second, then King of England, by whom she had issue Edward the 3rd, that succeeded his father to the crown of England. Now what did the barons of France when they saw that, following the right succession, of force they must become subjects unto England, the shame and servitude whereof could not in the Frenchmen be supported? They incontinently studied a remedy, and made a law that no heir female should inherit the crown of France; proceeding forthwith to the crowning of Philip de Valois, and after him of King John that followed. And so rested in peace a certain time until this Edward the 3rd, son of the said Isabel, came to the possession of England; who had no sooner the sword in hand, but into France he goeth, and there hewed and burned so long, that at length in plain battle he took this King John prisoner, and leading him into England, kept him there more than three years. Finally, seeing it impossible to govern France in peace, being King of England, he fell at a composition with the said King John for his ransom, besides the which for a memory of his interest, he reserved in the articles of record these two covenants: that is to say, that the French King and his successors should perpetually pay unto the crown of England 50,000 crowns, or thereabouts, of yearly tribute; and should have, and should leave also, the title of King of France unto the Kings of England; by authority whereof the King of England writeth unto this day himself *Rex Angliæ et Franciæ*, and the French King writeth *Rex Francorum*. And this tribute hath the French King foreborne to pay these sixteen or seventeen years past, so that I thought it worth the reckoning among other debts.'

'As you say,' said another of them, ' the honour is more worth than the money.'

'It is very true,' said I; 'but this will I speak against myself, that a good Christian ought not to fight, neither for money nor for honour. But where am I now? Good faith, I remember not well what resteth me to answer.'

'Marry,' said my Contrary, 'the marriage of the King's daughter, and the Duke of Norfolk's death.'

'Alas, alas!' said I, 'I am already tired; but because he that goeth to the battle loseth by his blood-shedding if he fight it not out, I will see how I can overcome this little rest with as few words as I may possibly.

'13. If I should say that the Lady Mary, the King's daughter that is, deserveth not a husband, I should surely prove a silly young man; and therefore will I now make you my judges; when for a stature of a woman's body she is neither too high nor too low; for beauty of face she hath few fellows that I know, and in proportion of members my pen cannot paint her. But what is all this? Nothing. For when I come to consider her virtue, her shadow maketh me to tremble—all the prudence, all the modesty, all the courtesy, all the sober smiling cheer that may be in a woman is surely in her; prompt in invention, awares in speech, learned in the tongues, perfect in music to sing and play; and on the lute and virginals, without master in all the world; yea, she is grateful to all persons, that I wot not what living creature were sufficiently worthy to describe her. So if a husband might be a reward unto the bounty of so gracious a lady, I will say she is and ever hath been worthy to have had the worthiest husband of the world. But now to the purpose of that her father would not consent she should marry (as I can imagine—not that I know this for surety) two several respects moved him thereto: the one, that to marry her to any one of meaner estate than her degree required, it should have been a great blemish to her and her honours; and the other, that to marry her to a high personage until his son, the King that now is, were established in his realm, it might have been occasion of some civil sedition or impediment of his son's quiet dominion. And were not, trow you, these considerations good?'

'Yea,' said my Contrary, 'since this son was born; but *before?*'

'Before,' said I, 'he ever hoped to have a son; and then, also, was his divorce fresh and new, which allowed him not at that time to dispose her in marriage. And this sufficeth of her Grace.

'14. Finally, unto the death of the Duke of Norfolk, and of his son, the Earl of Surrey, I must answer you by the same hearsay that you have opposed me; since, being in Italy, mine ears on matters of England have more power than mine eyes. Now, as I am informed, this Earl of Surrey, who was a young man, that after his father's death should have been the greatest lord in England next the King, seeing the King sickly and not like long to continue, imagined with himself how he might attain the crown. First, he considered well how the Prince was young, and not able to govern himself; and then he perceived how the multitude of inconstant people were diverse of

religion, some Protestants, some Papists; so that
with a little power of his friends he thought it
possible to draw one of these parties to him, and by
some foreign help to attain his purpose. But God,
that confoundeth the vain men in their vain
thoughts, brought these imaginations to knowledge
by means of some of his friends, to whom in figure
he had promised the coming of a fair day; which
words, revealed unto the King, and compared with
the suspected ambition of that young man, and with
other presumptions more than I know, caused his
Majesty more diligently to examine the matter;
insomuch that there were certain arms found set
forth by him the said Earl of Surrey, wherein the
royal arms of England were joined with his, and one
picture especially, in the which he had painted himself with the crown on his right hand and the King
on his left hand; so that when he was brought into
the open judgment he could not deny but that he
had devised means to bring his purpose to effect;
whereunto the duke his father was privy, who therefore incurred the semblable danger. But, as I hear
say, the King that is dead pardoned the old duke's
life; and I cannot hear for a truth he should be
dead. But if he were, I warrant you (said I) it is
not so without good cause; for a poor soldier that
came even now from the Emperor's camp, told me,
in Florence, not four days agone, that he had heard
a whispering among the soldiers, how that the said
Earl of Surrey, at his being with the Emperor
before Landrecey, was entered into intelligence with
divers great captains, and had gotten promise of aid
towards the furniture of his intent. 'Yea,' said

he, 'and further; he should have been the Emperor's man for the self-same purpose.' I will not say (quoth I), that this is true, but when the mean private soldiers are grown so commonly to talk of these things, it is to be presumed that amongst the great captains there should be somewhat of importance, for without some fire there was never smoke.'

'It is possible enough,' said one of them; 'for I myself, who have been in the Emperor's camp, have heard many reasonings of this matter, insomuch that it was doubted whether this young Prince were legitimate or no.'

'Legitimate!' said I, 'that were a doubt indeed; for I am sure there can no creature be legitimate if he be not. Do you not remember how I have showed you how the King that is dead, after the decease of his two first wives, was cleared unto all the world or ever he married the third wife, on whom he begat the young King Edward that now is; so that there can be no kind of reasons made against his legitimacy. Alas! (said I), if you knew the towardness of that young Prince, your heart would melt to hear him named, and your stomach abhor the malice of them that would him ill; the beautifullest creature that liveth under the sun; the wittiest, the most amiable, and gentlest thing of all the world; such a spirit of capacity for learning the thing taught him by his schoolmasters, that it is a wonder to hear say; and, finally, he hath such a grace of port, and gesture, and gravity, when he cometh into any presence, that it should seem he were already a father, and yet passeth he not the age of ten years—a thing undoubtedly to be much rather seen than believed. Alas! (quoth I); nay, alas! again; what cruelty should move these ravening dragons to covet the devouring of so meek an innocent lamb with the seditions of such devilish rumours?'

'No, no, I shall tell you why,' said my Contrary; 'the King was interdicted by the Church of Rome when he begat the Prince, and therefore, perchance it may be said his title is not good.'

'Good faith,' said I, 'and so may it be as well said that because the realm hath been this fifteen years no less interdicted than the King, therefore shall the earth bring forth no fruit; and yet, thanks be to God, since the world began we had never greater plenty of all things than we have had in this time, by so much the more as the idle bellies of the great multitude of our ancient religious persons have now no more license to devour, spoil and waste our ploughman's travail. But, believe me well, they that make them such a church of warm wax to serve all moulds, at length with changing of their figure, may happen to lose their form. How now (said I to my Contrary), are you satisfied?'

'Unto all your arguments, I am and I am not,' said he.

'I wot not how, by the holy mass,' said one of them who erst had spoken no words; 'thou hast quit thyself like a tall fellow; and if thou wilt go with me to dispute in a case of contumacy that I am called for before the Pope's legate, I will seek none other advocate, and thou shalt have a crown for thy labour.'

'I am no canonist, sir,' said I, 'nor cannot therein serve your purpose. *Quia non protestor protestationes appellandi.*'

'No,' said he, 'I will that you do no more than declare my reasons.'

'Reason!' quoth I, 'before the legate! That were a way indeed to bring me into limbo. Have I not told you that the Pope and all his ministers are express enemies to all good reason and verity?'

'In faith, in faith,' quoth my Contrary, 'if the legate did know of your reasoning here to-night, I would not be in your coat for another crown.'

'I know that well enough,' said I, 'for the least reward I should receive would be the result of one of these three—the sword, the prison, or the fire; and when well he had done his worst, because he can do no more than bring me to my death, the end of all my misery, and beginning of all my true joy, I would not greatly pass of his tyranny; remembering this saying of Job unto the Lord, 'Short be the days of man, and Thou hast with thee the number of his months; Thou hast ordained him his terms, which he cannot pass.' Nevertheless I will keep out of his danger as well as I may, for I will straight to Venice, where I trust to be free.'

'Nay, by our Lady,' said he, 'there are you deceived; for if you be known in Venice, the legate that liveth there will straightways have you by the back.'

'Why,' said I, 'is it possible that the famous liberty of that city should be in so much servitude that the lords thereof would suffer me for the just defence of my Prince to endure persecution under their wings; specially since the amity between them and my said King hath been so perfect, that when the Pope, with all the other princes of Europe, entered into a confederacy together for their destruction, our said King only remained their friend. But let God work His will, for I have determined in this case to trust more unto the justice of their first glorious commonwealth than to fear the tyranny of the Pope, who, under a counterfeit name, not only usurpeth the monarchy over the princes of the world, but also seeketh the blood of the poor labourers of the earth. And if you will find out a false knave by the changing of his right name, I will you do but mark this little title that I shall tell you. *Papa* in the Greek tongue, pronouncing the first syllable short, and the last long, is understanded a priest in the English tongue; and the Greeks unto this day call their priests *Pape;* so that *Pape* came first unto Rome as a poor private priest, none otherwise. But when, in process of time, after the priests had converted emperors, they began to take upon them temporal bishoprics, usurping all manner of worldly possessions and honours; then the glorious Bishop of Rome, being ashamed of so base a title as priest, made them pronounce the short syllable for the long, calling himself *Paapa* for *Papaa;* and so, with turning the wrong side outwards of a poor priest, he is grown to that glory that you see him in. And to prove again that he is no less a counterfeit in his doings than in his names, he writeth himself *servus ser-*

vorum Dei, whereas he in very deed serveth no true servants of God, but rather utterly persecuteth them. So that, to understand this title well, I can find no good interpretation, unless you would say that the devil's are God's servants, as the hangman is minister of the justice, who, for his own private gain, would hang all the men in the world if the justice would suffer him: and as the hangman useth the pliant halter to strangle withal the condemned persons, so may we say the devils, God's servants, use the popes as their ministers, to bring our poor souls unto perdition.

'But let me these trifles pass, to come unto a conclusion of our King, whose wisdom, virtue, and bounty my wits suffice not to declare: of personage he was one of the goodliest men that lived in his time, very high of stature, in manners more than a man, and proportionable in all his members unto that height; of countenance he was most amiable, courteous and benign in gesture unto all persons, and specially unto strangers; seldom or never offended with anything, and of so constant a nature in himself, that I believe few can say that ever he changed his cheer for any novelty how contrary or sudden soever it were. Prudent he was in council and forecasting; most liberal in rewarding his faithful servants, and ever unto his enemies as it behoveth a Prince to be: he was learned in all sciences, and had the gift of many tongues; he was a perfect theologian, a good philosopher, and a strong man at arms; a jeweller, a perfect builder as well of fortresses as of pleasant palaces; and from one to another there was no necessary kind of knowledge from a king's degree to a carter's but that he had an honest sight in it. What would you I should say of him? He was undoubtedly the rarest man that lived in his time. But I say not this to make him a god, nor in all his doings I will not say he hath been a saint; for I believe with the prophet, *non est justus quisquam, non est requirens Deum, omnes declinaverunt, simul inutiles facti sumus, non est qui faciat bonum, non est usque ad unum.* I will confess that he did many evil things as the publican sinner, but not as a cruel tyrant, or as a pharisaical hypocrite; for all his doings were open to the whole world, wherein he governed himself with so much reason, prudence, courage, and circumspection, that I wot not where—in all the histories I have read, to find one private king equal to him; who in the space of thirty-eight years' reign never received notable displeasure, how well that at one selfsame time he hath had open war on three sides; that is to say, with France, Scotland, and Ireland; insomuch that being in person with his army in France, he hath had a bloody battle stricken in the Borders, between him and the Scots, of 70,000 or 80,000 men, whereof his perpetual good fortune granted him most famous victory, with the triumph over his enemy the Scottish King, slain in that battle. And, finally, mark well this proof; the perfect present author for an extreme example of a happy man can allege no greater than *Polycrates Samian*, who for all his prosperous days, finished his life nevertheless in mischief in the cruel hands of his enemies; whereas this King Henry the 8th not only hath lived most happily, but also hath died most quietly in the arms of his most dear friends, leaving for witness of his most glorious fame the fruit of such an heir as the earth is scarcely worthy to nourish, who, I trust, shall with no less perfection reform the true church of Christ, not permitted by his said father to be finished, than as Solomon did the true Temple of Jerusalem, not granted to David in the time of his life. For who would speak against the dead King Harry might much better say he did see with but one eye, and so accuse him for lack of putting an end to the reformation of the wicked Church than for doing of the things he hath done against the apostolical Roman law. And who will consider well the discourse of the truth shall find the root of all the rehearsed mischiefs (if mischiefs they may be called) to have grown either in the bosom of the Pope, of the cardinals, and of their prelates and ministers, or else of those superstitious lay people, as they call them, who have borne more faith unto the members of the malignant Church than unto the true God Himself. So that to make a just exclamation, you ought to cry out against the exterminate tyranny of your whorish Mother Church, and say—Oh you Romans, oh Bollognese, oh Ravennates, or Parmesans, or Placentines, or Avignons, how can you thus abide, not only to be oppressed with so many customs, taxes, and tallages, that the poor can find no food, but also to have your .blood drawn even unto death? Oh commonwealth of Florence, why suffered thou Pope Clement to take from thee thy liberty? And thou Duke Cosmo di Medici, how canst thou suffer those friars of St. Mark, proved for open ribalds, to dwell in thine own house in thy despite? No, no, I will forbear to speak of any other things that I could allege as good as this; which indeed are so manifest, rebellions, or rather tyrannies, against their just and lawful Princes, that they cannot be denied, and yet is there no man that dare once speak or open his mouth against those ribalds. But it may chance the Turk will come one day to put the office of Christian Prince in execution, since they themselves will not attend unto it. How say you, my masters (quoth I), are these things true or not?'

'They be true,' answered they all; and passing from one matter to another whilst the time of supper approached, we fell into divers talk of things too long now to rehearse; and albeit, gentle reader, that unto the proof of my purpose in this one disputation, I did truly allege many more reasons than in this my little book are written, which, in case of scrupulous doubt, might perchance some time more perfectly have guided thee unto true knowledge, yet shall I beseech thee in that behalf not to accuse me of sloth; for my intent in this doing tendeth to none other but unto the just excuse of my wrongfully slandered Prince, whose good renown, fame, and honour, I most heartily commend unto thee.

And thus farewell.

NOTES.

NOTE A.

JUDGMENT was never pronounced in the Legates' Court; but the case arrived at a point where the sentence, if sentence were given, could only be in the King's favour; and the Emperor, to protect Catherine, was obliged to insist on the avocation of the suit to Rome.

The following letters add something to our knowledge of the influences which were at work below the surface. Inigo de Mendoza was a secret agent of Charles V. in England. De Praet, who became afterwards celebrated, was Minister at Rome.

Inigo de Mendoza to Charles V.

June 17, 1529. [MS. Archives at Brussels.]

When I left London the Queen's affair was hardly spoken of; the process was suspended. There seemed to be no occasion to enter protests or register appeals; and Campeggio was uncertain whether the Cardinal of York would consent to act under the commission. After arriving at Bruges, however, I heard that the King was again urgent for haste, and that the Queen had received a summons to appear before the Legates on the 28th of this present month. Her Majesty wrote on the instant to give notice to the Regent, and to beg that the two lawyers who were with her before might be sent over. English advocates, she said, would not speak for her with as much freedom as strangers. Notwithstanding this letter, my Lady the Regent thought, that inasmuch as her Majesty had pleaded that her cause could not have a fair hearing in that realm, the lawyers had better not go. I conceive myself, however, that the Queen of England desired their presence merely that they might decline in her name the jurisdiction of the Legates' Court, and allege for her the grounds of her objections. She will be distressed, as your Highness may suppose, when she finds that they do not arrive; and her friends will lose heart, and believe that she is abandoned. But my Lady the Regent may alter her mind. At present she thinks only of sending to Rome.

Dr. May has written to me of his interview with the Pope. He has sent me a copy of the protest which he has entered in the Queen's behalf. I should have forwarded it to your Highness were I not sure that you were already informed of everything. His Holiness is putting off the fulfilment of his promises till the last moment, and I fear that, notwithstanding the doubts which have hitherto been entertained about it, he may have directed the Legate to proceed on the first commission. Should this be so, your Majesty may consider the Queen's cause as lost. I have instructed her, however, through a notary, whenever the court threatens sentence, to appeal, and to demand to be heard at Rome, in arrest of judgment. If this is done, the sentence will be invalid; but I am afraid that she is deceived by her advisers. No doubt she has some good and true men about her, but there are others in whom I have little confidence; and for this reason it is most important that she should have the assistance of the lawyers. Not only is the Queen, as I have always assured your Majesty, a most devout and honourable woman, but she unites in her person a number of indirect advantages; and she deserves all the exertion which we can make, and all the assistance which we can render.

M. de Praet to Charles the Fifth.

Rome, August 5, 1529. [MS. Archives at Brussels.]

Unless I mistake, the majority of the cardinals are better disposed towards your Majesty than towards any other sovereign. Space will not permit me to repeat what they have said to me; suffice it that their words are all that you can desire. Dr. May has reported to your Majesty a conversation which he has held with some of them touching benefices and the like. I should say myself (and I have said it often before) that your Majesty may have the whole college at your devotion for ever if you will spend twenty thousand ducats among the leading cardinals in pensions and benefices. Give one of them a thousand, another two or three thousand, and you will find the money well laid out to your advantage.

The business of the Queen of England was despatched, as you will have heard, two or three days before my arrival. They have been so dilatory that I fear, before the 'avocation'

arrives in London, the King may have proceeded to some
scandalous act or other. Your ambassador was not to blame
for the delay. I have spoken to his Holiness. I have told
him that such conduct discredits the Holy See, as much as it
affects your Majesty. Pious Christians are offended, and the
Lutherans and heretics seek for nothing so much as an occasion
to calumniate his Holiness and the Papal chair.

A letter from the English ambassador here has been inter-
cepted. He writes largely, and, as it were, desperately, of the
whole business. We have shown it to his Holiness. Your
Majesty will find it in the present packet.

Note B.

With the avocation of the cause to Rome, the positions of
the Queen and King were reversed. Catherine declared that
she could not receive justice before the Legates in London.
Henry, with as much truth, asserted that there was no pre-
cedent for the appearance of a Sovereign Prince as a suitor in
the Papal Court. He could neither plead in person there, nor
acknowledge the lawfulness of the summons by deputing a
proctor, even were the case of such a nature that it could be
trusted to a proctor's management. The marriage question
merged itself into a discussion on the Papal privileges.

The King had from the commencement received the support
of the Court of France. Both Francis and his ministers encouraged him in a course which would separate England from
the Empire; and as eagerly they invited the Pope to make
concessions which would be an injury and an affront to Charles
the Fifth.

The next group of letters illustrate the successive aspects
which the struggle assumed before it ended in the Act of
Supremacy and the revolt of England from the Papal com-
munion.

The Cardinal of Lorraine to Cardinal —— at Rome.

Paris, Jan. 8, 1531-2. [MS. Bibliot. Impér. Paris.]

RIGHT REVEREND FATHER AND LORD IN CHRIST,—After our
most humble commendations—The King of England complains
loudly that his cause is not remanded into his own country;
he says that it cannot be equitably dealt with at Rome, where
he cannot be present. He himself, the Queen, and the other

witnesses, are not to be dragged into Italy to give their evidence; and the suits of the Sovereigns of England and France have always hitherto been determined in their respective countries.

Nevertheless, by no entreaty can we prevail on the Pope to nominate impartial judges who will decide the question in England.

The King's personal indignation is not the only evil which has to be feared. When these proceedings are known among the people, there will, perhaps, be a revolt, and the Apostolic See may receive an injury which will not afterwards be easily remedied.

I have explained these things more at length to his Holiness, as my duty requires. Your affection towards him, my lord, I am assured is no less than mine. I beseech you, therefore, use your best endeavours with his Holiness, that the King of England may no longer have occasion to exclaim against him. In so doing you will gratify the Most Christian King, and you will follow the course most honourable to yourself and most favourable to the quiet of Christendom.

From Abbeville.

Francis the First to Pope Clement the Seventh.

Paris, Jan. 10, 1531-2.   [MS. Bibliot. Impér. Paris.]

MOST HOLY FATHER,—You are not ignorant what our good brother and ally the King of England demands at your hands. He requires that the cognizance of his marriage be remanded to his own realm, and that he be no further pressed to pursue the process at Rome. The place is inconvenient from its distance, and there are other good and reasonable objections which he assures us that he has urged upon your Holiness's consideration.

Most Holy Father, we have written several times to you, especially of late from St. Cloud, and afterwards from Chantilly, in our good brother's behalf; and we have further entreated you, through our ambassador residing at your Court, to put an end to this business as nearly according to the wishes of our said good brother as is compatible with the honour of Almighty God. We have made this request of you as well for the affection and close alliance which exist between ourselves and our brother, as for the filial love and duty with which we both in common regard your Holiness.

Seeing, nevertheless, Most Holy Father, that the affair in

question is still far from settlement, and knowing our good brother to be displeased and dissatisfied, we fear that some great scandal and inconvenience may arise at last which may cause the diminution of your Holiness's authority. There is no longer that ready obedience to the Holy See in England which was offered to your predecessors; and yet your Holiness persists in citing my good brother the King of England to plead his cause before you in Rome. Surely it is not without cause that he calls such treatment of him unreasonable We have ourselves examined into the law in this matter, and we are assured that your Holiness's claim is unjust and contrary to the privilege of kings. For a sovereign to leave his realm and plead as a suitor in Rome, is a thing wholly impossible,* and therefore, Holy Father, we have thought good to address you once more in this matter. Bear with us, we entreat you. Consider our words, and recall to your memory what by letter and through our ministers we have urged upon you. Look promptly to our brother's matter, and so act that your Holiness may be seen to value and esteem our friendship. What you do for him, or what you do against him, we shall take it as done to ourselves.

Holy Father, we will pray the Son of God to pardon and long preserve your Holiness to rule and govern our Holy Mother the Church. FRANCIS.

M. de la Pomeroy to Cardinal ——.
London, March 23, 1531-2. [MS. Bibliot. Impér. Paris.]

MY LORD,—I sent two letters to your lordship on the 20th of this month. Since that day Parliament has been prorogued, and will not meet again till after Easter.

It has been determined that the Pope's Holiness shall receive no more annates, and the collectors' office is to be abolished. Everything is turning against the Holy See, but the King has shown no little skill; the Lords and Commons have left the final decision of the question at his personal pleasure, and the Pope is to understand that, if he will do nothing for the King, the King has the means of making him suffer. The clergy in convocation have consented to nothing, nor will they, till they know the pleasure of their master the Holy Father; but the other estates being agreed, the refusal of the clergy is treated as of no consequence.

---

* Chose beaucoup plus impossible que possible.

NOTE B.

Many other rights and privileges of the Church are abolished also, too numerous to mention.

In July, 1532, Henry and Francis agreed to meet at Calais and Boulogne, to arrange a common policy. The conference came off in October. Charles the Fifth, meanwhile, having done his worst to Henry, the latter had no objection to attack him, should opportunity offer, in Flanders. The Government at Brussels, it will be seen, were too well informed to be caught off their guard. Henry took Anne Boleyn with him to France, and originally intended to marry her during the conference.

—— *to Francis the First.*

Ampthill, July 23, 1532.   [MS. Bibliot. Impér. Paris.]

SIRE,—Your Majesty's promise to meet the King your brother, is in every way delightful to him. I have informed the Grand Master of the English proposals, but everything is referred to your own good pleasure.

In the recent treaty with the Germans, Sire, the King your brother thinks the Princes have the advantage of you; he supposes you to have undertaken to pay half their expenses: but he leaves this to be talked over with you. He spoke to me, as I told you a fortnight ago, of the inroad of the Turks. He wanted to know, I thought, whether they were instigated by your Majesty; so I told him you had nothing to do with them—you were a friend of King John of Hungary—and if the Turks were acting in concert with him, all would go well.

He answered at once that it was as he always thought. The Emperor might say what he pleased; but you and he were as good Christians as the Emperor, though not perhaps as good Papists.

He told me he had advices from Flanders that there were not a thousand soldiers left in that country—all were gone against the Turks. He bade me send you word, and ask, at the same time, how their towns were furnished. <u>I perceived, Sire, from his words, that he would be ready to play a game there,</u>* but his information I knew to be incorrect. Things are not in the condition for such an enterprise; so I dropped the subject, and left him without an answer. Sire, may God grant you a long and happy life.

---

* The words underlined are in cypher.

Charles the Fifth to the Regent Mary.
Mantua, October 16, 1532. [MS. Archives at Brussels.]

I found your packets on arriving here, with the ambassadors' letters from France and England. The ambassadors will themselves have informed you of the intended conference of the Kings. The results will make themselves felt ere long. We must be on our guard, and I highly approve of your precautions for the protection of the frontiers.

As to the report that the King of England means to take the opportunity of the meeting to marry Anne Boleyn, I can hardly believe that he will be so blind as to do so, or that the King of France will lend himself to the other's sensuality. At all events, however, I have written to my ministers at Rome, and I have instructed them to lay a complaint before the Pope, that, while the process is yet pending, in contempt of the authority of the Church, the King of England is scandalously bringing over the said Anne with him, as if she were his wife.

His Holiness and the Apostolic See will be the more inclined to do us justice, and to provide as the case shall require.

Should the King indeed venture the marriage—as I cannot think he will—I have desired his Holiness not only not to sanction such conduct openly, but not to pass it by in silence. I have demanded that severe and fitting sentence be passed at once on an act so wicked and so derogatory to the Apostolic See.

Captain Thouard to M. Dyce.
Gravelines, November 12, 1532. [MS. Archives at Brussels.]

SIR,—I have been unable hitherto to send you further information about the conference. But this evening Captain —— has come in with news.

The King of England did really cross with the intention of marrying; but, happily for the Emperor, the ceremony is postponed. Of other secrets, my informant has learned thus much. They have resolved to demand as the portion of the Queen of France, Artois, Tournay, and part of Burgundy. They have also sent two cardinals to Rome to require the Pope to relinquish the tenths, which they have begun to levy for themselves. If his Holiness refuse, the King of England will simply appropriate them throughout his dominions. Captain —— heard this from the King's proctor at Rome, who has been with him at Calais, and from an Italian named Jeronymo, whom the Lady Anne has roughly handled for managing her business badly. She trusted that she would have been married in September.

The proctor told her the Pope delayed sentence for fear of the Emperor. The two Kings, when they heard this, despatched the cardinals to quicken his movements; and the demand for the tenths is thought to have been invented to frighten him.

They are afraid that the Emperor may force his Holiness into giving sentence before the cardinal arrives. Jeronymo has been therefore sent forward by post to give him notice of their approach, and to require him to make no decision till they have spoken with him.

Threatened on both sides, the Pope did nothing: and Henry, though he had consented at the conference to postpone his marriage a short time longer, declined to wait beyond the winter, and made Anne Boleyn his wife about the 25th of January. Parliament met in February, and as it was now necessary to terminate somehow the suit for the divorce, the Act of Appeals was passed, abolishing the Papal jurisdiction.

The French Court, in the hope of still preventing the rupture, again laid a pressure on the Pope; while M. Chastillon, the ambassador in London, was instructed to implore the King to delay the publication of the Act. The King, it will be seen, was more inclined to moderation than his ministers. The immediate object was to induce Henry so far to recognise the Pope's authority as to send to Rome an 'Excusator;' some one who would 'excuse' his presence, and show why he could not plead there.

Chastillon to Montmorency.

London, March 6, 1533.   [MS. Bibliot. Impér. Paris.]

My Lord,—I have received your letter from Chantilly, dated the 24th of February, with another in cypher from M. de Paris, who gives me hope that the Holy Father will make concessions, and desires me on my part to do two things here—to prevent the King, if possible, from publishing the Antipapal resolutions passed in Parliament, and to persuade him to send over an 'excusator,' to be kept in readiness in the hospital at Rome in entire secresy.

I assure you, my lord, I have had enough to do. The

ministers in whom the King most confides are so opposed to our Holy Father that they raise every imaginable difficulty. They have failed, however, and that you may better understand what has taken place, you must pardon a somewhat long despatch.

The morning after I had communicated to the King the hopes entertained by M. de Paris, his Majesty sent for me and desired me to repeat my words before the council. I obeyed; but the majority declared that there was nothing in them to act upon, and that the King must not put himself in subjection. His Majesty himself, too, I found less warm than in his preceding conversation. I begged the council to be patient. I said everything that I could think of likely to weigh with the King. I promised him a sentence from our Holy Father declaring his first marriage null, his present marriage good. I urged him on all grounds, public and private, to avoid a rupture with the Holy See. Such a sentence, I said, would be the best security for the Queen, and the safest guarantee for the unopposed succession of her offspring. If the marriage was confirmed by the Holy Father's authority, the Queen's enemies would lose the only ground where they could make a stand. The peace of the realm was now menaced. The Emperor talked loudly and made large preparations. Let the King be allied with France, and through France with the Holy See, and the Emperor could do him no harm. Thus I said my proposals were for the benefit of the realm of his Majesty, and of the children who might be born to him. The King would act more prudently both for his own interest, and for the interest of his children, in securing himself, than in running a risk of creating universal confusion; and, besides, he owed something to the King his brother, who had worked so long and so hard for him.

After some further conversation, his Majesty took me aside into a garden, where he told me that for himself he agreed in what I had said; but he begged me to keep his confidence secret. He fears, I think, to appear to condescend too easily.

He will not, however, publish the Acts of Parliament till he sees what is done at Rome. The vast sums of money which used to be sent there out of the country will go no longer; but in other respects he will be glad to return to good terms. He will send the excusator when he hears again from M. de Paris; and for myself, I think, that although the whole country is in a blaze against the Pope, yet with the good will and assistance of the King, the Holy Father will be reinstated in the greater part of his prerogatives.

For the present all goes well. May it please your lordship to allow M. de Morette to join me here. A second person is required to observe, as well as myself.

The efforts of Chastillon and the Bishop of Paris were thwarted. Actions were stronger than words, and again and again when a hope seemed to offer itself of a reconciliation, either the Pope, or the King of England, or both, took some step which rent in pieces the efforts of diplomacy. A meeting was to take place in the coming summer between the Pope and Francis the First. The Duke of Orleans was to marry Catherine de Medici; and Francis flattered himself that he could bring Clement conclusively to the Anglo-French alliance. Within a few days of Chastillon's conversation, Clement issued censures against Henry, commanding him, on pain of instant excommunication, to separate from Anne Boleyn. Henry replied with publishing the Act of Appeals, and closing the long question of the divorce in an English court. Meanwhile Chastillon was recalled, and succeeded for a time by D'Inteville, the 'Bailly of Troyes,' a better Catholic than his predecessor, and a secret confederate, as he turned out afterwards, of the Papal faction.

D'Inteville to Francis the First.

London, May, 1533. [MS. Bibliot. Impér. Paris.]

SIRE,—The King your brother bids me tell you that you should, in his opinion, give notice to the Germans of this intended interview (with the Pope.) They may otherwise suspect you of meaning something to their disadvantage; and fearing a change on your part towards them, they may fall off themselves to the Emperor.

The English ambassador in Paris sends him word, he tells me, that your Majesty fears the alterations introduced by the Act of Appeals may retard this interview, and create fresh difficulties. He says that he cannot help himself. The Pope forces him to publish the Act by the censures which have been unjustly issued against him. The Pope is acting towards him neither as a friend nor as an impartial judge, but with an open enmity, against which he must defend himself as he can.

You will hear more at length about things from the Duke of Norfolk; meanwhile the King has given me the enclosed list of his grievances. The Archbishop of Canterbury will try the divorce cause, and sentence will be passed in about three days. I entreated that he would wait at least till the Holy Father should arrive at Nice, but he would not consent. I asked him to keep the sentence secret, so that the Pope might not hear of it till he had seen your Majesty. The King answered, 'Impossible; the sentence must be published and generally known before the Queen's coronation, and she is to be crowned at Whitsuntide.'

The Queen is *enceinte*. The child is to be the heir of the crown, and he will not leave it in the Pope's power to decide against its legitimacy. He says, too, that it will be more honourable to the Pope to accept the decision of the Archbishop of Canterbury, than to pass sentence himself.

D'Inteville to Cardinal Tournon, Ambassador at Rome.
London, June 9, 1533.   [MS. Bibliot. Impér. Paris.]

MY LORD,—The King of England desires me to write to you in the same terms in which I have written to our Sovereign Lord and to the Grand Master.

It has been declared in Rome, in full Consistory, that the Most Christian King intends to employ his powers against the Lutherans; and that, if necessary, he will invade them in person. The King of England is marvellously displeased. If our Sovereign Lord relinquish the intelligence which has been commenced with the Germans, all Europe, he says, will fall into the hands of the Pope and the Emperor. You cannot conceive how angry he is. He calls the Most Christian King the worst adviser and the worst friend in the world. As to the interview, our Sovereign Lord, he says, is too anxious for it. If all were meant fairly, the Pope would be more eager than the Most Christian King, and the many smooth words between them indicate something underhand.

I did my best to soothe him. I said that our King only desired the interview through his affection to his Majesty, and as to manœuvres there were none unless for the marriage of which he had been informed long since.* But I never saw him so angry. The news from Rome I suppose are the cause. They have written to say that the Pope still makes delays, and will do nothing of importance—that is, will pass no sentence —before the interview. If the sentence, when it is given, be against his wishes, I doubt whether the King will find his people

---

* Between the Duke of Orleans and Catherine de Medici.

as obedient as they might be. He is acting prudently in attaching the nobles and the great men to himself, that the people when they rise may be without head or leader. If God please, things will not come to that point; but you know the English people; when they have the will to rebel, they do not stay to calculate chances.

The Pope replied to Cranmer's sentence with fresh menaces. The King of France wrote to remonstrate, and on the 17th of August Cardinal Tournon answered thus:—

Cardinal Tournon to Francis the First.

Rome, August 17, 1533. [MS. Bibliot. Impér. Paris.]

SIRE,—I have delivered your message to his Holiness on the affair of the King of England, and I have told him how much you were annoyed at the step which had been taken. His Holiness said that he was sorry to have acted contrary to your wishes, but the King of England obliged, and in a manner drove him to it. The King of England was not content with disregarding briefs and inhibitions, and taking a wife, but he had published laws in derogation of his Holiness's authority and of the rights of the Holy See. The Archbishop of Canterbury had usurped the office of judge, and, in his sentence, a copy of which was read in the Consistory, he called himself *Legatus Natus* of that very See which he was outraging.

In fact, Sire, as I have told you before, the cardinals would have been in despair of the Pope had he acted otherwise. But however it be, your Majesty can still do much for the King of England, if you can keep the Duke of Norfolk with you till the Pope's arrival. As I hinted in my last letter, little as the King of England seems inclined to undo his work and submit to the Holy See, the Pope will do for him with the utmost readiness all that can be attempted in honour. It may be that, when you are together, his Holiness will light on some expedient.

The Pope spoke fairly, but, like a rower in a boat, his face was one way, his movements were another.

He followed up his threats with censures, declaring Henry *ipso facto* excommunicate.

Francis again wrote in indignation to insist that the censures should be suspended, and on the birth of Elizabeth in September, permitted his ambassador in England to attend the baptism.

Cardinal Tournon to Francis the First.

Rome, September 27, 1533. [MS. Bibliot. Impér. Paris.]

SIRE,—Incontinently on the receipt of your letter requiring the suspension of the censures against the King of England, I waited on his Holiness and earnestly entreated his compliance. His Holiness answered that for himself he would do anything in his power, so great was his regard for your Majesty; but your demand was of a kind which he could grant only in Consistory, and he found that the cardinals would make a difficulty. I begged his Holiness, in your name, to do his best to persuade the said cardinals. Your motive, I said, was simply the hope that the approaching interview might have good effects.

At last, Sire, his Holiness consented to use his influence with them, and he did it so successfully that not one of them said a word in opposition.

The censures, therefore, were suspended by the Consistory yesterday.

The interview between the Pope and Francis the First came off at Marseilles at the end of October. Henry was to have been represented there by the Duke of Norfolk; but Norfolk was recalled on the first issue of the censures. Dr. Bonner attended in his place, but only to present an appeal on behalf of the King of England from the Pope to the next general council. The appeal was rejected; but the Pope promised, that if Henry would submit to be represented by a proctor, and acknowledge the Pope's right to try the cause at Rome, he would give judgment in his favour. Henry believed, and perhaps rightly, that the Pope was playing him false. If the Pope could promise to give judgment for him, the Pope must have satisfied himself that his cause was just; why then so many conditions and delays ? The marriage of the Duke of Orleans with Catherine de Medici while his own business remained unsettled, aggravated his suspicions. The reports of D'Inteville and Chastillon on the King's feelings and on the condition of the country become now highly curious.

NOTE B.

D'Inteville to Montmorency

Greenwich, November 7, 1533.　　　　[MS. Bibliot. Impér. Paris.]

MY LORD,—You will have seen my letter to his Majesty, and the report of my conversation with the King. He was on the way from his room to chapel to hear mass. He stopped as he passed me, and tried to make me believe that I had been instructed to tell him that the marriage of the Duke of Orleans should not come off until the Pope had despatched his business as he desired.

I assured him that he was mistaken, that I had told him no such thing, nor had been directed to tell him; and I offered to show him my instructions. He replied, that although I had not said it, the King had said it, and said it to himself; nor was he the only witness; for the same words had been used to the Queen at Calais.

He then left me, and as he turned to the altar added, that if the marriage took place while nothing had been done for him, he would have small reason to thank the King's friendship.

While he was at mass, I went to the Duke of Norfolk's room to finish my letter, for which the courier was waiting. I had no opportunity of speaking with the King again after the service, but I had a long conversation with my Lord of Norfolk.

The King, I said, was marvellously importunate with our master. He must be aware that our master was taking more pains in this business than he had taken for himself and his children; and if his trouble and his expense (for the money it cost him was no trifle) were to be so ill acknowledged, he would not be very well pleased. I desired the duke and some other influential members of the council who were present to tell the King what I said, and to tell him also that, if he went on thus he might tire out our master's patience. If they were true friends to the King of England, I said, they ought to be glad to see the Most Christian King on good terms with the Pope. The closest alliance which our master could form with the Pope's Holiness would be the best in the end for their master. If the Most Christian King were to act as their master would have him act, the Pope's Holiness would throw himself unreservedly on the Emperor, and their master's prospects would not be mended.

I assure you, my lord, many of the council agreed in what I said most fully, especially the Duke of Norfolk, who did not scruple to tell me so; but the duke said that the whole business had so inflamed and irritated the King their master's brain, that he did not trust one of them. He was himself, he said, one of those in whom the King had most confidence, but both King and Queen often held him in suspicion. Believe me, my lord, there are some here, and those of the greatest in the land, who will be indignant if the Pope confirm the sentence against the late Queen. There is little love for the one who is Queen now, or for any of her race.* My lord, I hear that M. Chastillon is again in England. On Sunday I shall present him to the King, and myself take my leave. Before I go, I shall speak my mind plainly to his Majesty. The lords of the council will hardly tell him the truth as roundly as I shall do.

D'INTEVILLE.

Notes of the Complaints of the King of England, apparently in D'Inteville's hand.
November, 1533.   [MS. Bibliot. Impér. Paris.]

He complained that all Christian princes now knew the alliance between France and England to be no longer what it was. The division between them was everywhere notorious.

As to the innovations which the King of France undertook that the King his brother should not make, the King said he had kept promise, and his honour was untouched. The Pope began by issuing censures, and by refusing to admit his reasons for declining to plead at Rome.

He complained that he was required to send a proctor. He was told that the cause should be decided in favour of whichever party was thus represented; but he said that for the sake of all other sovereigns, as well as himself, he would send no proctor, since, by so doing, he would acquiesce in the rejection of his excuser. The laws passed in Parliament, he declared, were for the welfare of the commonwealth, and he would not suspend them. The King of France had told him that the Pope admitted his cause to be just. The French lawyers unanimously affirmed the same, and he was therefore astonished that the Most Christian King should now advise him to let a proctor go.

If the Pope complains of injuries which the Holy See has

---

* Underlined in the original.

received from England, the Pope has injured England in turn, and has been the first to begin. The question of injuries had better be dropped on both sides. The King says that he demands no reparation, nor will he make any reparation. He asks only for justice; and if he cannot obtain that justice, it is enough for him that he has God and right on his side, as the Pope has admitted.

He complained of all this prodigious humility and kissing of feet, so unlike what was promised him at Calais, so unlike the 'want of confidence' which was then to be the rule with the Pope. His advice had not been followed—faith had not been kept with him. The marriage was not to have been contracted till the Pope had done justice.

He complained of the French council, who overpersuaded the Most Christian King against his better judgment. They wished to deal with him, also, he supposed, in French fashion, playing with him, and entertaining him with false hopes, and cheating him after all. But he was not a man to be toyed with thus—he had known the world too long. He himself spoke what he meant, and he would have others speak as they meant. Those who would deal frankly with him, he would stand by with life and goods, but otherwise he would not; and his friendship, he thought, was of another sort than the Pope's, and better worth.

As to the interview, he had been told that ——* was talked of. He said that he could hardly believe it; but whatever was done, it would be only trifling, and instead of drawing the friendship closer, would weaken it. He had not mentioned the interview before for two full months.

Moreover, he said, that for himself his council do not govern him, but that he governs his council. He desires their opinions, but the resolution is with himself, and every King ought to do the same. He bade me give his best respects to our master, and tell him that he still hoped the Most Christian King would be his good brother and friend. In spite of appearances hitherto to the contrary, he would not yet give up his confidence.

At the end of all this, he bade me say something. I answered that the King his brother had never ceased to exert himself in his behalf; that the Most Christian King, he might be assured, never took so much pains for himself or his children when in captivity.

---

* Word illegible in MS.

He began again, and went to the other end of the room to M. Chastillon, to whom he said the truth was plain enough. The Most Christian King, he repeated again and again, was no longer the friend to him which he had been. The French council were entangling him with their affection for the Pope.

For his own part, he declares that he will never more acknowledge the Pope in England. He will allow him as Bishop of Rome, or as Pope (if he so please to be called), but he will concede him no more authority over himself or his subjects; and he will be none the worse Christian for that, but rather the better. Above all things, and in all places, he will acknowledge Jesus Christ as the only Lord of Christian men. Christ's word, he says, shall be preached in England, and not the canons and decrees of Popes. He professes to have heard from his ambassador at the Court of the Emperor that the Spaniards will come and make war upon him. But he says he has no fear of them. They may come to England if they will; they may find it not so easy to return.

The Queen sends her regards to his Majesty, and trusts that he will give proofs of the affection which he has professed to feel for her, as she in turn will do him service as occasion may offer.

Chastillon to the Bishop of Paris.

Greenwich, November 17, 1533. [MS. Bibliot. Impér. Paris.]

MY LORD,—M. d'Inteville returns to-morrow. I will add, at present, but one word on the state of things here.

The King of England falls away every day more and more from the friendship which he once felt for our King. He supposes our King to have neglected his interests with the Pope, and to have shown little value for the English alliance.

He has made up his mind to a final and complete revolt from the Holy See. He says that he will have the 'holy word of God' preached throughout the country; and our Lord, he believes, will aid him in defending his rights.

It is a bad business, and a bad example to other princes. He is determined, however, and the lords about the court and the greater part of the people go along with him.

May the Creator grant you a long and happy life.

Your humble servant,

CHASTILLON.

In the beginning of the ensuing year, Parliament passed the first Act of Succession, determining the crown to the children of Anne Boleyn. The Pope's authority was conditionally abolished, with a proviso, however, that he might have three months to consider himself; and the Nun of Kent and her accomplices were attainted. Henry, at the same time, threatened to form a Protestant league, and the Bishop of Paris started for Rome to make one last effort to preserve the peace.

But it was too late. On the 23rd of March the Pope gave final sentence in the divorce cause. The King of England was enjoined to take back Queen Catherine within four months, or he was declared excommunicate. His subjects were absolved from their allegiance: and the Imperialists undertook to execute the censures, invade England, and depose the king.

D'Inteville to M. de Tarbes.

October, 1534. [MS. Bibliot. Impér. Paris.]

MY LORD,—You will be so good as to tell the Most Christian King that the Emperor's ambassador has communicated with the old Queen. The Emperor sends a message to her and to her daughter, that he will not return to Spain till he has seen them restored to their rights.

The people are so much attached to the said ladies that they will rise in rebellion, and join any prince who will undertake their quarrel. You probably know from other quarters the intensity of this feeling. It is shared by all classes, high and low, and penetrates even into the royal household.

The nation is in marvellous discontent. Every one but the relations of the present Queen, are indignant on the ladies' account. Some fear the overthrow of religion; others fear war and injury to trade. Up to this time, the cloth, hides, wool, lead, and other merchandize of England have found markets in Flanders, Spain, and Italy; now it is thought navigation will be so dangerous that English merchants must equip their ships for war if they trade to foreign countries; and besides the risk of losing all to the enemy, the expense of the armament will swallow the profit of the voyage. In like manner, the Emperor's subjects and the Pope's subjects will not be able to trade with England. The coasts will be blockaded by the ships of the Emperor and his allies; and at this moment men's fears are aggravated by the unseasonable weather throughout the summer, and the failure of the crops. There is not corn enough for half the ordinary consumption.

The common people, foreseeing these inconveniences, are so violent against the Queen, that they say a thousand shameful things of her, and of all who have supported her in her intrigues. On them is cast the odium of all the calamities anticipated from the war.

When the war comes, no one doubts that the people will rebel as much from fear of the dangers which I have mentioned, as from the love which is felt for the two ladies, and especially for the Princess. She is so entirely beloved that, notwithstanding the law made at the last Parliament, and the menace of death contained in it, they persist in regarding her as Princess. No Parliament, they say, can make her anything but the King's daughter, born in marriage; and so the King and every one else regarded her before that Parliament.

Lately, when she was removed from Greenwich, a vast crowd of women, wives of citizens and others, walked before her at their husbands' desire, weeping and crying that notwithstanding all she was Princess. Some of them were sent to the Tower, but they would not retract.

Things are now so critical, and the fear of war is so general, that many of the greatest merchants in London have placed themselves in communication with the Emperor's ambassador, telling him, that if the Emperor will declare war, the English nation will join him for the love they bear the Princess.

You, my lord, will remember that when you were here, it was said you were come to tell the King that he was excommunicated, and to demand the hand of the Princess for the Dauphin. The people were so delighted that they have never ceased to pray for you.* We too, when we arrived in London, were told that the people were praying for us. They thought our embassy was to the Princess. They imagined her marriage with the Dauphin had been determined on by the two Kings, and the satisfaction was intense and universal.

They believe that, except by this marriage, they cannot possibly escape war; whereas, can it be brought about, they

---

* The marriage between Mary and the Dauphin had been proposed some years before. It was the occasion of the doubt raised by M. de Tarbes of Mary's legitimacy. The reopening of the question came from the Emperor, who hoped to bribe Francis to join him against England, and compel Henry, by force or fear, to acquiesce.

will have peace with the Emperor and all other Christian princes. They are now so disturbed and so desperate that, although at one time they would have preferred a husband for her from among themselves, that they might not have a foreign King, there now is nothing which they desire more. Unless the Dauphin will take her, they say she will continue disinherited; or, if she come to her rights, it can only be by battle, to the great incommodity of the country. The Princess herself says publicly that the Dauphin is her husband, and that she has no hope but in him. I have been told this by persons who have heard it from her own lips.

The Emperor's ambassador inquired, after you came, whether we had seen her. He said he knew she was most anxious to speak with us; she thought we had permission to visit her, and she looked for good news. He told us, among other things, that she had been more strictly guarded of late, by the orders of the Queen that now is, who, knowing her feeling for the Dauphin, feared there might be some practice with her, or some attempt to carry her off.

The Princess's ladies say that she calls herself the Dauphin's wife. A time will come, she says, when God will see that she has suffered pain and tribulation sufficient; the Dauphin will then demand her of the King her father, and the King her father will not be able to refuse.

The lady who was my informant heard, also, from the Princess, that her governess, and the other attendants whom the Queen had set to watch her, had assured her that the Dauphin was married to the daughter of the Emperor; but she, the Princess, had answered it was not true—the Dauphin could not have two wives, and they well knew that she was his wife: they told her that story, she said, to make her despair, and agree to give up her rights; but she would never part with her hopes.

You may have heard of the storm that broke out between her and her governess when we went to visit her little sister. She was carried off by force to her room, that she might not speak with us; and they could neither pacify her nor keep her still, till the gentleman who escorted us told her he had the King's commands that she was not to show herself while we were in the house. You remember the message the same gentleman brought to you from her, and the charge which was given by the Queen.

Could the King be brought to consent to the marriage, it would be a fair union of two realms, and to annex Britain to the crown of France would be a great honour to our Sovereign; the English party desire nothing better; the Pope will be glad of it; the Pope fears that, if war break out again, France will draw closer to England on the terms which the King of England desires; and he may thus lose the French tribute as he has lost the English. He therefore will urge the Emperor to agree, and the Emperor will assist gladly for the love which he bears to his cousin.

If the Emperor be willing, the King of England can then be informed; and he can be made to feel that, if he will avoid war, he must not refuse his consent. The King, in fact, has no wish to disown the Princess, and he knows well that the marriage with the Dauphin was once agreed on.

Should he be unwilling, and should his wife's persuasions still have influence with him, he will hesitate before he will defy, for her sake, the King of France and the Emperor united. His regard for the Queen is less than it was, and diminishes every day. He has a new fancy,* as you are aware.

The Emperor entered warmly into the project for marrying Mary to a French prince—the Dauphin, or one of his brothers —and in November the Count de Nassau went to Paris to see what could be done.

Charles V. to his Ambassador at Paris.

November, 1534. [MS. Archives at Brussels.]

. . . . In addition, the Count de Nassau and yourself may go further in sounding the King about the count's proposal—I mean for the marriage of our cousin the Princess of England with the Duke d'Angoulesme. The Grand Master, I understand, when the count spoke of it, seemed to enter into the suggestion, and mentioned the displeasure which the King of England had conceived against Anne Boleyn. I am therefore sincerely desirous that the proposal should be well considered, and you will bring it forward as you shall see opportunity. You will make the King and the Grand Master feel the importance of the connexion, the greatness which it would confer on the Duke d'Angoulesme, the release of the English debt which can be easily arranged, and the assurance of the realm of France.

Such a marriage will be, beyond comparison, more advantageous to the King, his realm, and his children, than any

---

* Il a des nouvelles amours.

benefit for which he could hope from Milan; while it can be brought about with no considerable difficulty. But be careful what you say, and how you say it. Speak alone to the King and alone to the Grand Master, letting neither of them know that you have spoken to the other. Observe carefully how the King is inclined, and, at all events, be secret; so that if he does not like the thing, the world need not know that it has been thought of.

Should it be suggested to you—as it may be—that Anne Boleyn may be driven desperate, and may contrive something against the Princess's life, we answer that we can hardly believe her so utterly abandoned by conscience: or, again, the Duke of Anjou may possibly object to the exaltation of his brother; in which case we shall consent willingly to have our cousin marry the Duke of Anjou; and, in that case, beyond the right which appertains to the Duke and Princess from their fathers and mothers, they and either of them shall have the kingdom of Denmark, and we will exert ourselves to compose any difficulties with our Holy Father the Pope.

NOTE C.

The attitude of the foreign Powers, the insurrectionary spirit in England, and the intrigues so largely carried on between the disaffected Catholics and the agents of Charles the Fifth, led to the Act of Supremacy. The plea for the intended rebellion against Henry was to be the Papal excommunication. By the Act of Supremacy every man, on pain of death, was compelled to disclaim the Pope's pretence to absolve subjects from their allegiance, and to accept and admit the supreme sovereignty of the King in Church and State. Under this Act Fisher and More were executed. Paul the Third, who had succeeded Clement, invited the Catholic Powers to avenge their deaths and the wrongs of the Holy See.

Paul the Third to Francis the First.

July 26, 1535. [MS. Bibliot. Impér. Paris.]

DEARLY BELOVED IN CHRIST,—Health and our blessing. We committed to your Majesty the defence of the Cardinal of Rochester, and from your excellent goodness, and from your influence with Henry, King of England, we promised ourselves that we should speedily hear of his release. We are now shocked to learn that, after a long imprisonment, he has been put to death. We doubt not that, after your earnest, though, alas! unavailing efforts in behalf of the said cardinal, your Majesty feels deeply how atrocious is this deed. Your Majesty's intercession not only failed, but seems to have hastened the catastrophe. But we, my son, we and this Holy See, what must we feel when the Church of Christ is thus lacerated! Shall we mourn for his innocence and piety, his wisdom, his zeal for the Catholic faith, so famed throughout the world? Shall we deplore the outraged dignity of a prelate and cardinal? Shall we lament his cruel death—a fate befitting a traitor inflicted on a saint? These things are all most miserable; but saddest of all is the cause for which he died. He offered up his sainted life for God, for the Catholic religion, for justice, and truth. He persisted, not like St. Thomas of Canterbury, in defence of special and peculiar privileges, but in behalf of the whole Church; and therefore this Henry has not only repeated, but far outdone, the evil deeds of his ancestor, both in the rank of the person slain, and in the weightiness of the cause. To the grievous ulcers already eating into his soul, he has added this the last and worst. He has despised the censures launched upon him by our predecessor. For two whole years he has continued in insolent and notorious adultery, causing public scandal in the Church. He has sacrilegiously murdered our clergy and friars. He has been guilty of heresy and schism, in rending away his realm from obedience to the Apostolic See. And now, last of all, when this most excellent prelate had for his wisdom and holy life been promoted to the dignity of a cardinal, he first tempted him to deny the truth, and when he could not prevail, he caused the blessed saint to be put to a public and shameful death by the hand of the executioner.

He slew him the more readily, because he had heard that we had named him cardinal. And thus, among his manifold enormities, this King has committed the crime of high treason, and has incurred, *ipso facto*, the legitimate penalty of deprivation.*

Other enormous deeds also he has dared to perpetrate, no lighter than those of which we have spoken. We are not ignorant how, at the late conference at Calais, he tempted you, most pious and worthy Prince, with accursed proposals, fraught with ruin to the Church. He was not ashamed to assail your virtue

---

* In accusing Henry of high treason, *læsæ majestatis*, the Pope advanced precisely the claim which the Act of Supremacy was designed to meet.

with his perfidious counsels, which, however, were by you deservedly repelled.

As his conduct towards you has been full of evil, so has yours been most excellent. Therefore for now three years, partly in regard for your Majesty, partly in the hope that Henry might repent, the Holy See has endured these iniquities at his hand. But her forbearance has availed nothing. Her patience under his crimes has rather invited fresh oppression; and we are now called, as by the very voice of God and the outcries of mankind, to take vengeance. With grief of mind, but driven by necessity, and supported by the unanimous counsel of the holy fathers of the Church, we now proceed to those measures which the cause of God and man enjoins upon us. This Henry, who, by rebellion, by heresy, by schism, and other enormous crimes, and now at last by the iniquitous murder of a cardinal, has rendered himself unworthy of his realm and dignity, we do declare deposed. Your Majesty, we doubt not, being a most Christian Sovereign, and most unlike to him in all things, holds those his deeds in abhorrence; we are assured that, mindful of God, the Church, and your duty, you will consider him unworthy of your alliance; that you will not look on him as King, but as usurper of the name of King. With you, therefore, dearly beloved in Christ, the Holy Church seeks for that refuge, which not in vain she has sought with your forefathers. We cast ourselves and our necessities upon your piety ; and we entreat you, remembering how mightily in times past your ancestors avenged the wrongs of Holy Church, to execute our sentence upon the said Henry, when by ourselves you shall be invited to take arms.

Thus much we commit to letter, the bearer of which, our nuncio, will confer with your Majesty at greater length on our behalf. To his words we refer ourselves; and to your Majesty's protection we commend the dignity of the Apostolic See and the honour of Almighty God.

Given at Rome, under the Fisherman's ring, July 26, 1535, the year of our Pontificate I.

Eustace Chappuys to Chancellor Granvelle.
[Decyphered Copy.]
London, November 21, 1535.   [MS. Archives at Brussels.]

SIR,—Considering my duty, the desire of the person you know of, and the importance of the cause, I suppose I ought

NOTE C. 107

not to have made any fresh demand in the affairs of the good
ladies. The King is so blinded, and so given over to a repro-
bate sense, that we may look to see God permit him to entangle
himself deeper and deeper in the devil's labyrinth. He will
make himself more and more abominable in the sight of mankind, and thus come to utter ruin and destruction. He talks
of providing a number of harquebusses, but they will not save
him, and he must look for them in some other place than
Flanders : but the intention means something ; he wishes probably to awe his subjects into quiet, and prepare against
foreign invasion.

Sir, Master Cromwell, of whose origin and antecedents
your Secretary Antoine tells me you desire to be informed, is
the son of a poor blacksmith, who lived in a small village four
miles from this place, and is buried in a common grave in the
parish churchyard. His uncle, the father of a cousin whom
he has since enriched, was cook to the late Archbishop of
Canterbury. The said Cromwell, in his youth, was an ill-condi-
tioned scapegrace. For some offence he was thrown into prison,
and was obliged afterwards to leave the country. He went to
Flanders, and thence to Rome and other places in Italy.
Returning after a time to England, he married the daughter of
a wool-comber, and lived in his father-in-law's house, carrying
on the business. Afterwards he was a law-pleader, and thus
became known to the Cardinal of York, who, perceiving his
talents and industry, and finding him ready at all things, evil or
good, took him into his service, and employed him in the demolition of five or six religious houses. On the cardinal's downfall Cromwell acquitted himself towards him with marked
fidelity, and afterwards fell under the displeasure of Sir John
Wallop, now ambassador in France, who threatened him with
violence.

Not knowing how else to defend himself, Cromwell contrived with presents and entreaties to obtain an audience of
the King, whom he undertook to make the richest sovereign
that ever reigned in England. He promised so fairly that
the King at once retained him upon the council, although his
promotion was for several months kept a secret from the
rest. Since that time he has risen above every one, except it
be the lady, and the world says he has more credit with his
master than ever the cardinal had. The cardinal shared his
influence with the Duke of Suffolk and several others. Now
there is not a person who does anything except Cromwell.
The Chancellor is only his tool ; and although he has, so far,

refused to take the Great Seal himself, people say he will be persuaded to catch at it before long.

He can speak his own language remarkably well, and Latin, French, and Italian tolerably. For the rest, he is a person of good cheer, gracious in words and generous in actions; his equipage and his palace are magnificent. My servant can tell you more if you wish for further information.

Sir, the person mentioned in my letter to his Majesty, has told me that the King, speaking to some one four or five days ago of the Princess, said that he would soon provide for her in such a way that she should need neither household nor company, and she should serve as an example to show the world that no one should disobey the law. He said that there was a prophecy about him that at the beginning of his reign he would be gentle as a lamb, and at the end worse than a lion; and he would prove the prophet true. The person I speak of, feels so uncertain what he may do, that he has sent to beg me not to put off the ladies any more with smooth words. He will himself, he told me, give them notice to look to themselves, and warn them they had better send immediately to the Emperor's Majesty.

On the 7th of January, 1536, Queen Catherine died, and Mary's chief anxiety was then to escape from England, as a preface to the Emperor's intended declaration of war.

Chappuys to Charles the Fifth.

Feb. 10, 1536. [MS. Archives at Brussels.]

SIRE,—Yesterday arrived the personage sent by M. de Rœulx to examine the plans for the enterprise, and to instruct me in the order to be taken. I fear, for the reasons which I stated in my last letter to your Majesty, the opportunity is gone. I have not, however, as yet received the answer of the person whom the affair concerns, and as that answer shall be, we will act to the best of our ability. Your Majesty shall have notice in time.

Chappuys to Charles the Fifth.

Feb. 17, 1536. [MS. Archives at Brussels.]

SIRE,—In my letter of the 10th I informed your Majesty of the arrival of the person despatched by M. de Rœulx, and I forthwith sent notice to the Princess by her confidential servant. The servant returned yesterday with an answer, that I need not keep her informed in detail of the plans for carrying her off; she left the whole arrangement to my discretion, having entire confidence in me, and I was to settle everything; she herself would be in readiness to leave the house, and this she thought she could do if we would provide her with a sleeping draught for the women who were placed about her; she would have to pass the window of her governess; but once outside the house she could find means to unlock or break open the door of the garden.

Sire, her anxiety to escape from her present unhappy situation is so great that I think if I told her to go to sea in a sieve she would do it, and this makes me fear that her eagerness blinds her to the difficulties of the enterprise. When the experiment is tried, those difficulties will be found more considerable than she anticipates, and she has no person of experience to advise her. If the house in which they have placed her be really so easy to leave, they may have purposely laid the temptation in her way, that they may have an excuse for treating her more harshly. She believes that there is no guard; but a guard there may be, notwithstanding, without her knowledge, as there was last year at Greenwich.

Sire, her present residence is for many reasons less convenient than the house where she was before. It is fifteen miles further from Gravesend, and at Gravesend M. de Rœulx says that she must embark, the mariners not caring to venture further up the river. She would have forty miles to ride, which she could not accomplish without relays of horses, and do what we would, I think she could not escape being detected and overtaken. The town adjoining is full of men and horses, and there are towns and villages along the road where she might easily be discovered and stopped.

Doubtless, could she be brought below Gravesend as the captain desires, the rest would then be easy; but the difficulty is the distance she must ride. If she embark near London, there will be danger on the passage down before she can be brought clear of the river. The captain says, among other excuses, that the scrutiny is so close that he cannot venture to bring any men with him below deck. There is no real obstacle here, however; the men might be dispersed in other vessels and landed at Gravesend, where they could rejoin him. The Princess thinks, and I learn the same thing elsewhere, that about Easter she will be removed again, perhaps to the old house, or it may be even nearer.

Nevertheless, Sire, ardently as the Princess longs to escape from her trouble, she would deem it far better and far safer that something should be undertaken of a larger kind, and a general remedy be devised for the service of God, for the salvation of the unnumbered souls which are now going the way to perdition, and for the repose and tranquillity of Christendom. Supposing her carried off, which will not be without difficulty and hazard, the question will not be settled. She says herself that stronger measures may be required, and the victory perhaps, after all, might then be less easy to achieve. The King is now off his guard; the realm is undefended, and he scarcely thinks of making preparations. Her escape might drive him to despair, and with the help of his money he might do many things.

For my own part, I think if the Princess were once in your Majesty's hands, the King would drop his bravado, and would not kick against the pricks. The Princess at any rate never ceases to entreat me to implore your Majesty to take up the matter promptly and swiftly; events move too slowly for her; and when the time comes she is prepared for death. She wishes me to despatch a messenger expressly to solicit your Majesty; in fact, she would have had the late Queen's physician go, were he willing to leave England. But I urged that in doing so she would show some distrust of your Majesty's good will; I assured her that the opportunity was watched for with the utmost vigilance, and I satisfied her that I ought not to send. I persuaded the physician to stay where he was, by telling him that the Princess might require his help, and could trust no one but himself. The King sent him to attend upon her. I spoke myself about it after the Queen's death; and the King gave permission that he should have access to her apartments at all times and seasons.

Report says, Sire, that a number of the old servants of the Queen her mother are to be transferred to the Princess's household, especially the head groom of the chamber, who is to hold the same office. Should this turn out true, there will be far less difficulty in carrying her off; the groom of the chamber being a man of ability—as fit a person for such a business as could be found anywhere. If only she return to her old house at Easter, so much the better, also. The time will be more convenient. The King at that season is usually at a distance, and the sea will be less dangerous.

Should it be determined finally to make the attempt, it will not be for your Majesty's honour that I should remain here;

for all the world will not be able to persuade the King that I was not the contriver and promoter of the business, and things might, perhaps, go hard with me. He has a large opinion of his own greatness, and he would like to show that he neither fears nor regards man; his concubine hates me because I have always told him the truth, and opposed his accursed obstinacy; and, as soon as the preparations are complete, I had better hasten off, with two or three of my people, to make a tour in Flanders. As I am known to have communicated with M. de Rœulx's servant, it is next to impossible that he should not discover my hand; if he find me out, he will certainly destroy me; while my going away may, perhaps, divert their attention.

Your Majesty will let me know your pleasure, and I will forthwith obey you. I will only beseech your Majesty not to impute what I have written to a want of will or courage. I am ever ready to die in your Majesty's service.

The Emperor, when Chappuys's letter reached him, was no longer in a condition to respond to Mary's expectations. In the midst of his designs upon England he was overtaken by a rupture with France; and, instead of encouraging the Princess to escape, and defying her father, he made the death of Catherine an excuse for burying the quarrel, he sent to Henry to court his alliance, and requested him to forget the differences of the last few years.

Instructions to D'Inteville and De Tarbes.

April 29, 1536. [MS. Bibliot. Impér. Paris.]

Since the departure of M. d'Inteville for England, the Most Christian King has received a letter from M. de Tarbes, dated the 19th of this month. He has therefore drawn these present instructions to serve alike for the Bishop and for M. d'Inteville, and to advertise them what they shall say to the King of England on the Most Christian King's behalf. And first:—

M. de Tarbes has informed the King of the arrival of a courier from the Emperor at the English Court, of the causes which induced the King of England to grant him an audience, of the language used towards him, on his arrival, by the Duke of Norfolk, and of the assurances given to M. de Tarbes, that whatever overtures the Emperor might make to the King of

England, the present relations between France and England would remain unaffected.

This last declaration has given the Most Christian King unfeigned pleasure.

In like manner, M. de Tarbes informs the King of the annoyance expressed by the King of England at the non-arrival of the person whom the Most Christian King was to send over, with the answer thereto made by M. de Tarbes ; which answer the Most Christian King thought so good that it did not need another word.

M. de Tarbes states, that in his letter to the King of England, the Emperor brings forward five points. In the order in which these points are arranged by the bishop—

The first declares that the Emperor was about to enter Rome.

The second relates to the invasion of Savoy by the King of France. The Emperor requests the King of England to intercede with the King of France for the restoration of the Duke of Savoy's dominions.

In the third, the Emperor expresses a fear that the Most Christian King will make war upon him for the Duchy of Milan; and, in that event, requests assistance from the King of England.

In the fourth, the Emperor desires the King of England to consent to forget what has passed between them on account of his late aunt. The occasion having ceased to exist, the Emperor hopes that the King of England will put away his suspicion and resentment, and will return to the old terms of cordial friendship and alliance.

In the last, the Emperor says he is about to send an army against the Turks, and he invites the King of England to co-operate with him against the enemy of the Christian faith.

On all these points the King of England has explained himself to the Bishop of Tarbes and to M. d'Inteville. His Majesty is especially pleased with the sage and prudent answer given by the King of England to the Emperor touching the Duchy of Savoy. The said bishop and M. d'Inteville are to thank the King warmly on his Majesty's behalf, and to thank him also for so graciously communicating to them the contents of the Emperor's letter.

His Majesty has been made to entertain the greatest possible confidence in the King of England's regard and affection.

The insurrection so long threatened broke out at last in

October, 1536; but, unfortunately for the prospects of the insurgents, at a time when the state of the Continent no longer permitted the Emperor to assist or countenance them. An emissary of the Flemish Court, in sending an account of the first successes of the rebels, in vain pointed out that the opportunity which had been waited for was come.

———— *to her Majesty the Queen Regent.*
London, October, 1536.   [MS. Archives at Brussels.]

MOST NOBLE LADY,— I am instructed to inform your Majesty that on Monday, the 2nd of this present October, in the northern counties in the diocese of Lincoln, the King's officers and commissioners were proceeding with the demolition of four abbeys, when certain peasants, by God's will, commenced a riot under the conduct of a brave shoemaker named William King.* The chief commissioner, Doctor Lee, who was especially obnoxious to the people, as the summoner who cited the late Queen your aunt, now in glory, before the Archbishop of Canterbury, contrived to escape; but his cook was taken, and, as a beginning, the people hanged him. A gentleman belonging to the Lord Privy Seal, otherwise called Master Cromwell, tried to stop them; and he too was immediately laid hands on, wrapped in the hide of a newly-killed calf, and worried and devoured by dogs; the mob swearing they would do as much for his master.

The people went next to the house of the Bishop of Lincoln, whom they could not find; but they caught his chancellor, and to spite the bishop, who is said to have been the first person to advise the King to divorce your aunt, they killed him.

The next day being Tuesday, there were more than ten thousand of them in arms; and they proceeded to take the gentlemen of the neighbourhood, and swear them to be true to their cause. The cobbler assumed a cloak of crimson velvet, with the words embroidered in large letters upon it,

FOR GOD, THE KING, AND THE COMMONWEALTH.

Some of the gentlemen who had been sworn escaped and gave notice to the King, and on Wednesday, at nine in the morning, an order came out that all the gentlemen in London should place themselves under the command of Richard Cromwell. The Lord Mayor undertook to provide horses, and

---

* Nicholas Melton was the name of the man who was called Captain Cobbler.

I

went in person from stable to stable, borrowing on all sides from natives and foreigners alike. To appease the complaints which began to be heard, it was given out that the horses were required for the Count of Nassau, who, they pretended, had come over with a train of men as ambassador, and had nothing to mount them on. On Saturday the number of insurgents had risen to fifty thousand, and there were said to be as many as ten thousand priests among them, who never ceased to stir them on to their work, and to tell them what great things they would achieve. The same day Lord Clinton's retinue joined them; Lord Clinton himself (it was he who married the Duke of Richmond's mother) had to fly with a single servant; and many other gentlemen were forced to fly also, who intended to have done service for the King.

When these news reached London, the King called a council; and immediately after the meeting, the Dukes of Norfolk and Suffolk, and the other lords, dispersed in different directions, as it was said, to prevent the insurrection from spreading. The admiral and Sir Francis Brian went down to Ampthill, and collected about ten thousand men out of Northamptonshire and the counties adjoining. On Sunday the King was said to be going to Ampthill also, and the royal standard was expected to be displayed. Sunday afternoon I saw thirty-four of the falconets which the King has been making during the last year leave the Tower of London. There was no shot or powder, however, that I could see, and they were badly provided with artillerymen. The next day, when they were drawn out of the City, the horses were found so bad, that, for want of better, thirteen of the guns went but a mile, and then returned to the Tower; while the remainder were taken but a small distance.

Men are hired, as many as can be obtained, in Kent and elsewhere; but the chances are that when in face of the enemy they will turn their coats, and join the rebels in their good quarrel. Those who have risen say they will live like their forefathers; they will maintain the abbeys and the churches, and pay no more imposts and subsidies. They demand the repayment of the sums which they have been forced to contribute already, especially the great loan exacted from them in the cardinal's time; and, finally, they will have surrendered into their hands the wool-comber (by whom they mean Cromwell), the tavern-keeper (which is their name for the Archbishop of Canterbury), and divers other bishops and lords of the council.

It was reported in London on Monday that the Earl of Northumberland's brother had joined the Commons with thirty thousand men. He wanted lately to be declared the earl's heir; the King made difficulties, and he now means to be revenged. It was also said that a number of other lords and great men had been forced to join, by a threat that they should have their houses pillaged; this has been done already with the houses of those who, after taking the oath, have deserted to the King. A priest and a shoemaker were stated to have been hanged the same morning for merely saying it was a pity to collect an army to put down such poor people. The King declared that they cared more for a set of rascals than for him.

Thursday morning a knight went down to the coast to fetch off the workmen employed by the King. The town of Sandwich also has provided sixty poorly furnished men-at-arms. The frontiers are now unprotected, and a landing can be easily effected. Even the French tailors in London are pressed to serve. They give them harquebusses and two groats a-day, making four ducats the month, for their pay, with a groat to drink for every five miles* they march. The Flemish shoemakers are made to go on the same terms. To the English they give but sixpence a-day, with the same drink money as they allow the French.

Madame, it appears to the person who has been sent to me by your Majesty, that it is good fishing in troubled waters; and that now, in these disturbances, there is an opportunity such as there has not been these hundred years, to take vengeance upon the schismatic for the wrongs which he has done with his French alliances to his Majesty the Emperor, for the injuries of your late aunt, his lawful wife, and for the iniquitous treatment of his patient daughter the Princess. A portion of the army now in readiness in Zealand would suffice to restore the Princess to her place and rank. Two thousand harquebuss men (it is of those that the need is greatest) should be landed at the mouth of the river which runs from York.

---

* *Cinque milles*, which, however, is incredible. The strongest ale then made was twopence a gallon, and to drink two gallons every five miles would have been beyond mortal capacity. The letter from which I transcribe is a copy, so that there is room to suppose a mistake. 'Cinque,' I think, should be cinquante, and for 'five' we should read fifty.

NOTE D.

—— to ——

London, May 16, 1536.   [MS. Archives at Brussels.*]

Lord Rochfort, brother of the wicked Queen Anne Boleyn, has been beheaded with an axe on a scaffold in front of the Tower.

The said lord made a good Catholic address to the people. He said that he had not come there to preach to them, but rather to serve as a mirror and an example. He acknowledged the crimes which he had committed against God, and against the King his sovereign; there was no occasion for him, he said, to repeat the cause for which he was condemned; they would have little pleasure in hearing him tell it. He prayed God, and he prayed the King, to pardon his offences; and all others whom he might have injured he also prayed to forgive him as heartily as he forgave every one. He bade his hearers avoid the vanities of the world, and the flatteries of the Court which had brought him to the shameful end which had overtaken him. Had he obeyed the lessons of that Gospel which he had so often read, he said he should not have fallen so far; it was worth more to be a good doer than a good reader. Finally, he forgave those who had adjudged him to die, and he desired them to pray God for his soul.

After Lord Rochfort came Mr. Norris, first gentleman of the bedchamber to the King; next to him Weston and Brereton, gentlemen of the bedchamber also; and then Mark the musician. These four said nothing except to pray for God's and the King's forgiveness, and to bid us pray for their souls. Brereton and Mark were afterwards quartered.

The wicked Queen herself suffered last on a scaffold within the Tower, the gates being open. She was led up by the lieutenant, feeble and half-stupified [elle etoit foible et etonnée], and she looked back from time to time at four of her ladies by whom she was attended. On reaching the platform she prayed to be allowed to say something to the people. She would not speak a word, she said, which was not good. The lieutenant gave permission, and, raising her eyes to heaven, she begged God and the King to forgive her offences, and she bade the people pray God to protect the King, for he was a good, kind, gracious, and loving Prince. This done, they removed an ermine cloak which she had on,

---

* Partially printed by Gachard, *Analectes Historiques*.

and she herself took off her head-dress, which was in the English fashion. One of her attendants gave her a cap into which she gathered her hair. She then knelt; a lady bound her eyes, and incontinently the executioner did his office. When the head fell, a white handkerchief was thrown over it, and one of the four ladies took it up and carried it away. The other three lifted the body, and bore it with the head into the adjoining chapel in the Tower.

It is said that she was condemned to be burnt alive, but the King commuted the sentence into decapitation.

Extract from a Letter of the Regent Mary to Ferdinand of Austria.
May 23, 1536. [MS. Archives at Brussels.*]

The English, I think, will not give us much trouble, especially now that we are quit of that damsel who was so good a Frenchwoman. You have no doubt heard that she has been beheaded, and in order that vengeance should fall on her from the subjects of his Majesty the Emperor, the King sent for the headsman from St. Omer's to do the work. There was no one in England skilful enough.

The King has, I understand, already married another woman, who, they say, is a good Imperialist. I know not whether she will so continue. He had shown an inclination for her before the other's death; and as neither that other herself, nor any of the rest who were put to death, confessed their guilt, except one who was a musician, some people think he invented the charge to get rid of her. However it be, no great wrong can have been done to the woman herself. She is known to have been a worthless person. It has been her character for a long time.

I suppose, if one may speak so lightly of such things, that when he is tired of his new wife he will find some occasion to quit himself of her also. Our sex will not be too well satisfied if these practices come into vogue; and, though I have no fancy to expose myself to danger, yet, being a woman, I will pray with the rest that God will have mercy on us.

Note E.

After Jane Seymour's death, both Charles and Francis affected an anxiety to secure the vacant hand of Henry. The

* Printed by Gachard, *Analectes Historiques*.

Imperial candidate was the Duchess of Milan. Among the many ladies at the French Court whose names were mentioned to him, Henry's fancy inclined to the only one whom he could not obtain, the Duchesse de Longueville. The Duchesse de Longueville, or Mary of Guise, had engaged herself to James of Scotland. M. de Chastillon, the ambassador in England, was occupied in endeavouring to persuade the King to content himself with one of her sisters, or with a daughter of the house of Lorraine or of Vendosme. The King, who had, perhaps, seen her, would have accepted the Duchesse de Longueville upon the spot. Chastillon's correspondence relates his efforts, at once fruitless and grotesque, to induce Henry to select either of the others. The King said he would not choose a wife in the dark, or act in such a business on another man's judgment. The young ladies must be sent to Calais, and he would go over and see them.

The French Court were anxious to keep him from the Duchess of Milan; and yet they could not consent to trot out their Princesses, as Montmorency said, like horses at a fair. If the King chose none, they would be all made ridiculous; and whether he made a choice or not, to send them to Calais on such an errand was disrespectful and discourteous. Chastillon's last letter on the subject will serve as a specimen of the rest.

Chastillon to Francis the First.

August 12, 1538. [MS. Bibliot. Impér. Paris.]

SIRE,—On Wednesday, the 9th of this month, I received the letter which you were pleased to write to me from Villa Franca, and I have laid before the King your brother the letter which preceded it, dated from Vienne the 28th of July.

I already knew from M. de Lassigny the terms on which you stood with the Emperor; and I had therefore anticipated the instructions with which you have now favoured me. I entreat your pardon if I have listened too readily to things told me here. I am not, I assure you, too well inclined to give credence to English rumours; but they were so positive in their story, and it tallied so nearly with my information from other quarters, that not having then heard from yourself, I may hope for your forgiveness. Dismiss me from your service if, in future, I let them use such language to me.

Sire, my last conversation with the King your brother followed on the delivery of your letter. I wished to keep him in as good a humour as I could, and without asking favours of him, I have somewhat improved his spirits. He has not been easy since he heard from De Lassigny that you were certainly friends with the Emperor, and he liked still less De Lassigny's going to Scotland. I have assured him, however, that notwithstanding the cordial friendship now established between your Majesty and the Emperor, he would always find you as well disposed to him as in times past. Your Majesty, I said, hoped that on his side he would be the same to you; and if you could be of any service to him with anything in your realm, you would be at his command.

'Well, well,' said he, 'but the King sends no message about the marriage.'

'Saving your presence, Sire,' said I, 'he writes that he does not think it honourable, as I have always told you, to send the young ladies to Calais. Send yourself some person or persons whom you can trust, and act on their report.'

'*Par Dieu*,' he replied, ' I will trust no one but myself; marriage touches a man too nearly. I will have them sing to me a few times before I settle.'

With a half smile I answered, 'Your Majesty would, perhaps, like to try them all, one after the other, and keep the one that suits you best. It was not thus, Sire, that the Knights of the Round Table treated their ladies in old times in this country.'

I think I made him ashamed; he laughed and coloured; and you will see at the end of my letter that he perceived he had been wanting in courtesy.

Rubbing his nose a little, he said,

'But since the King my brother is on such good terms with the Emperor, what, after all, will become of his alliance with me? I ask, because I am resolved not to marry at either Court, unless the Emperor, or the King my brother, prefer my alliance to that which they have made with one another.'

'By our Lady, Sire,' replied I, 'your question demands a wiser man than I am to answer it. Do you think if you marry the Duchess of Milan, the Emperor will prefer you to the King my master?'

'Yes, to be sure,' said he; 'I am certain of it.'

'Would you like me to tell the King my master this?' said I.

'*Par Dieu*, yes,' said he; 'for it is true.'

'Sire,' I said, 'I have no commission to answer such questions. You must tell your ambassador at my master's Court to ask the King.'

'*Par Dieu*,' he replied, 'I will do nothing of the kind till I have Doctor Bonner there for ambassador. The others have been led astray by Wyatt; they are not honest, and I am ill pleased with them.'

'Indeed, Sire,' said I, 'the Bishop of Winchester and Sir Francis Brian will have no pleasant time over there. Complaints have been made to me very unlike yours. I do not know what has been the matter, but they have behaved ill to us.'

The King then begged me to write to you to learn your intentions, and to let him know.

Wishing him to see that he was of no great consequence to your Majesty, I replied,

'Sire, I will speak to you frankly and openly. I am of opinion that you press too hard upon the King your brother. For the last ten years, as you are aware, he has never been at war but by his own choice: and, since he is willing to remain on the same friendly terms with you as before his agreement with the Emperor, I would advise you to accept his offers. He is a great and powerful sovereign, and the relations in which you stand with him are of no small moment to you. The King of Scots is as much at his beck as if he were his son; the King of Denmark is devoted to him; and France, Scotland, and Denmark are your near neighbours. If my master break with you, the other two will break also, and of what will happen you are a better judge than I. Secure his friendship if you will be guided by me, and do not look too closely into niceties.'

I went no further, being without instructions from your Majesty. Had there been time, I should have urged him to relinquish the pension, but this can be done hereafter if you please to direct me. I spoke as I did to put him out of conceit with his notion of a preferential alliance, on which he seemed inclined to insist; and also to make him feel that without looking to find five feet upon a sheep, your friendship was of as much consequence to him as his could be to your Majesty. I mixed some bitter with the sweet, because he never forgets his own greatness and thinks so little of others.

Shaking his head, and as it were thinking aloud, he answered, '*Par Dieu*, I have good subjects, and a good trench about me' [*j'ai de bonnes hommes et de bonnes fossez.*]

Then he added, that since you, Sire, were unwilling to let the ladies come to Calais, he would ask you to fix upon some place—the chateau of Madame de Vendosme, for instance, or any other house not far from Calais. No one need know the cause of the visit. The Duke of Guise might go with them as if on business of State, while he would himself send persons of equal rank with the duke to see them.

This time he said nothing about preference. You will understand, Sire, the terms on which I parted from him. I cannot tell whether he will do as the King of Scots did, and go in person to see for a wife. He certainly said he would trust no opinion but his own, and two or three times he begged that the place selected might be near Calais. Moreover, I do not know who in this country, except himself, is the equal in rank of the Duke of Guise. However, this is but guessing. At all events, unless he change his mind, he will send the most considerable persons to be found in the realm.

May it please you, Sire, to let me hear what further answers I shall give the King. The ladies that he means are Mademoiselles de Vendosme, de Lorraine, and de Guise. The younger of the two Mademoiselles de Guise has been much spoken of here, and in my opinion she it is that he will prefer. He thinks highly of the birth and breeding of the Guise family.

Note F.

The author of the Dialogue goes beyond his knowledge in his account of the divorce of Anne of Cleves. She was very far from beautiful; the King's distaste for her was from the first emphatic; and the marriage did not go beyond the ceremony.

Thomas, perhaps, never saw Anne, and may have seen instead Holbein's portrait, the instrument by which the King was deceived. He may have judged of Henry's regard from the splendid settlement which was made upon the Queen on the separation, and from the easy terms on which they afterwards continued. The real story was of a kind which could not be communicated to the world.

The history of the connexion, so unfortunate in itself, so scandalous in its consequences, is related in a series of letters from Marillac, Chastillon's successor as resident and minister in England. The reconciliation between Charles and Francis in the summer of 1538 was followed by an energetic effort on the part of the Pope to enlist them in a joint crusade against

England. Reginald Pole was sent to Spain to work on the Emperor; and his brother with Lord Montague, and the Marquis of Exeter, prepared to move at home as soon as war should be declared. The domestic treason was discovered, and the conspirators were executed: but preparations on a large scale were commenced in Flanders. After Lord Exeter's execution, Chastillon suddenly demanded his passports, and left the country. Eustace Chappuys, the Flemish ambassador, followed his example; and through February, March, and April, nothing was looked for in England but immediate invasion. Forts and bulwarks were thrown up along the coast. The musters were called out; the beacons were trimmed; the highways swarmed with armed men; and every morning was expected to reveal an enemy's flotilla at anchor in the Downs.

The promptitude of the King, the unexpected acquiescence of the country in Lord Exeter's death, and perhaps some difference at the last moment between the Emperor and the French King, arrested the action of the Catholic coalition. Chastillon's departure was explained away, and at the end of March M. Marillac was sent over to take his place. The internal condition of England on his arrival; the subsequent endeavours of Cromwell to oppose a Protestant league to the Catholic; the marriage with Anne of Cleves, intended as an indissoluble link between England and Germany, and proving in the end a most fatal cause of disunion; the desperate measures to which Cromwell's failure drove him, and his final arrest and fall, together form the subject of a correspondence too interesting to be mutilated.

Marillac to the Constable.

April 3, 1539. [MS. Bibliot. Impér. Paris.]

MY LORD,—I sent you word from Boulogne of the causes which had delayed my departure. The weather when I sailed was so wild that I was two days and a half at sea, and it was not till the 28th of last month that I reached London. The council were absent, and the King made me wait three days before I could be admitted to an audience to present my letters.

The King, my lord, is in marvellous distrust as well of the King our master, as of the Emperor. He is confident that they intend to declare war against him; and he is therefore taking measures with the utmost haste for the defence of the realm. He foresees that if attacked at all, he will be attacked in force, and he is calling under arms the whole strength of the realm. As I passed through Dover I saw new ramparts and bulwarks on the rocks which face the sea. They had all been made since the return of M. de Chastillon, and were well furnished with artillery, large and small. No landing at Dover could be attempted now with a prospect of success.

In Canterbury, and the other towns upon the road, I found every English subject in arms who was capable of serving. Boys of seventeen or eighteen have been called out, without exemption of place or person. The inhabitants of London are formed into a corps by themselves for the protection of the City. French subjects residing here for trade have not been spared; they too have been required to serve, whether they desire it or no. Some have answered bravely that they would not bear arms against their natural Sovereign. Others, taken unawares, have yielded through timidity.

On the road I met a body of men. I was told there were six thousand of them, going as a garrison to Sandwich. As I approached the City I saw the King's ships and galleys all armed and ready to sail. A multitude of private vessels were fitting at their side with all speed; and when this flotilla goes to sea, and unites with the five-and-twenty or thirty ships at Portsmouth, the whole force will amount to a hundred and fifty sail.

Merchants' traffic outward or inward is interdicted. Every vessel is under arrest, and no one is allowed to leave the realm. English subjects abroad have received orders to return, and are most of them by this time at home. Artillery and ammunition pass out incessantly from the Tower, and are despatched to all points on the coast where a landing is likely to be attempted. In short, my lord, they have made such progress that an invading force will not find them unprovided. They are prepared on all sides to the very extent of their ability, and the great lords are at their posts as if the enemy were already at their doors.

The cause of the excitement, my lord, is a conviction on the part of their King that the Emperor, the Pope, and our master, are in a league to destroy him and his realm. The King told me himself that he knew from the best authority that the Most Christian King was concerting measures with the Emperor to fall upon him. Your secretary, my lord, he said, was waiting in Spain to bring you the Emperor's latest instructions. M. de Chastillon's sudden departure gave a show of reason to the alarm. The Emperor's ambassador demanded his passports directly after, and went away without speaking of a successor; and where before there was little doubt that mischief was meant, the uncertainty was then at an end. They looked for nothing but immediate hostilities.

At this moment there is especial agitation on account of the appearance of sixty sail of Flemings, said to be on their way to Spain for the expedition to Algiers. People here do not believe that Algiers is their real destination. They are vessels of large burden, unsuited to the Levant, and the impression is that they are transports. Fifty or sixty more have been discovered by scouts in the harbours of Zealand, and report says that they have ten thousand men on board them.

These things have placed the King upon his mettle. He has sent troops northward, for he looks to be invaded over the Scottish Border. But his preparations are defensive merely, not aggressive. He will never choose such a time as the present to meddle with his neighbours of his own will, or to seize and fortify any second Calais on the French coast. As matters stand, his great anxiety is to be on friendly terms with our master, for never was our master's friendship of more importance to him.

My lord, when I was at Boulogne I heard that the Dean of Cambray was to be Flemish ambassador, and that he had arrived at Calais. He reached London two days after me. I have not seen him because he has not yet had audience of the King, but I shall not fail to visit him immediately on his reception.

Marillac to Francis the First.

April 15, 1539. [MS. Bibliot. Impér. Paris.]

At this moment there are not less than from eighty to a hundred ships of war ready for action. The musters of London will be reviewed on St. George's day, and the King is expected to be present. The expense, so far, of the fortifications, arms, ships, etc., must amount to two hundred thousand crowns at least.

Marillac to the Constable.

April 15, 1539. [MS. Bibliot. Impér. Paris.]

MY LORD,—They are mustering, drilling, and fortifying their exposed frontiers in all directions. They think of nothing else. The Dukes of Norfolk and Suffolk, with the other great lords, are away in their counties, providing for the public safety. My lord, no invading force could show itself without the whole nation being warned, and every man will be ready to march wherever danger threatens. Most of the ships have already sailed. Those which remain are chiefly the property of private persons, English or foreign; but there are very few of them which are not in fighting order. Lord Cromwell has ten thousand men twenty-five miles off; and next Friday, St. George's day, will be the review in London. There will be from fifty to sixty thousand men, perhaps, for not a man who can bear arms is excused. The foreigners resident have received orders to provide weapons and to appear in the City livery. Indeed, my lord, they are thoroughly prepared; and on the sea, although they have now but a hundred or a hundred and twenty ships, they say they will shortly have a hundred and fifty. Considering the time they have been at work, they have not done badly.

Marillac to the Constable.

May 1, 1539. [MS. Bibliot. Impér. Paris.]

MY LORD,—You will understand by my letter to the King the satisfaction with which his despatch was received here. The whole Court seems to have received good news. Men's faces are all altered for the better; and, if one may judge their feelings by their outward demonstrations, I should think they are satisfied that for this year, at least, they will be let alone. Our King's letter and yours, as I am told, have been read out in Parliament. In return for my good news, they give me a better reception, and, great and small, caress me with all their might. The King himself talked to me for two long hours, and I perceived by his words that for the present they are out of alarm.

My lord, I must not omit to tell you that the King is again showing an inclination for the Germans. The Duke of Saxe's chancellor, with a deputation from some of the other States, has just arrived. Some say the King's daughter is to be married to the Duke of Saxe's son; others, that they are coming to an ·agreement in religion at last. Nothing certain can be known till it is seen how things will go in Parliament, and to the proceedings there, my lord, I shall attend closely, and send you information at length.* The fortifications and the other preparations for war continue, but they are doing their work more soberly, and at their leisure. The great review in London has gone off. Such a spectacle was never seen here before.

The Constable of France to Marillac.
May 13, 1539. [MS. Bibliot. Impér. Paris.]

Lord Cromwell demands the release of the Bibles printed here in the English vulgar tongue.

I imagine that before you left Paris you were made acquainted with the answer which we have given to the reiterated demands of the English minister. The King has been informed that there are many errors in the translation, and he will not countenance the issue of it. What is good can be printed in England as well as in France; what is false his Majesty will not allow to be printed here. He will lend no colour nor authority to the publishers to put out bad things. This is our answer.

Marillac to Francis the First.
May 20, 1539. [MS. Bibliot. Impér. Paris.]

SIRE,—The Government continue to throw up works wherever an enemy can land, though they are going on more slowly. They have made up their fleet to a hundred and twenty sail, which will carry ten thousand men. The whole nation, as I have already told your Majesty, is under arms. At the late review in London I counted about fifteen thousand English, without reckoning foreigners. They were in white uniform from head to foot, and ten thousand of them were well found in all points.

The Parliament, Sire, is in full session; but as yet we cannot say certainly what will be done. They have been busy so far in finding money to meet the cost of the defences. There has been some difficulty about the abbeys. A party here wish to apply the monastic estates to the foundation of new bishopricks, educational colleges, and hospitals for the poor. Objections have been taken, too, touching the prosecution of the ladies who are prisoners in the Tower—the wife of the

---

* Parliament met on the 27th of April.

NOTE F.

Marquis of Exeter the King's cousin, and the mother of Cardinal Pole, who is also one of his relations. Their sentence, however, is daily expected, and from present appearances it will go hard with them.

Marillac to the Constable.

May 20, 1539.   [MS. Bibliot. Impér. Paris.]

MY LORD,—After the reply which you were pleased to make to Lord Cromwell's request for the release of the Bibles, they have said no more to me about the matter; and I have not myself cared to reopen it. If Lord Cromwell demands a further answer, I shall reply in the words of his Majesty's council to the English ambassador.

The Parliament, I am told, is likely to separate without having arrived at a resolution on some points, and it will reassemble in September. Sentence of death, however, will probably be passed against the ladies of whom I spoke in my letter to the King, and against a gentleman and a chaplain of the late marquis's household. In three or four days they will be brought from the Tower to Westminster to be condemned. This is a serious matter. I have not thought well to write more fully to the King about it until I could tell him the exact truth; but persons who profess to know assure me that it is as I have said; and unless the King pardon them, so the event will prove.

Marillac to Francis the First.

June 9, 1539.   [MS. Bibliot. Impér. Paris.]

SIRE,—Your Majesty desires to be informed of everything which passes in this country. At present I have nothing to add to my late letters unless it be that, whereas a few days since it was thought that Parliament would rise at Whitsuntide and be prorogued till September, the King, immediately after the holidays, said it must sit on till St. John's day, and finish the business which had been taken in hand. Several points, therefore, points especially affecting religion, have now been brought to a conclusion. The bishops have had a grand struggle. Part desired to maintain the mass complete, part to make a new service. The majority were with the conservatives, who have carried the day. The King, as the leader of this party, said all which ought to have been said. He maintained that the Holy Sacrament ought to be believed and adored, and to be honoured with the ceremonies observed in the church from immemorial time. Evil speaking, therefore, against the sacrament is prohibited under pain of death; and priests, to the great displeasure of the ambassador of Saxe, are forbidden to marry—so angry was he that he went off two days since in the worst imaginable humour.

The appropriation of the abbey lands and the fate of the ladies in the Tower, will be disposed of before Parliament now separates. The ladies are the mother of Cardinal Pole, and the wife of the late Marquis of Exeter. The two Houses have attainted them of high treason, and according to the custom of the country, their goods are confiscated and their lives are at the King's mercy.

Marillac to the Constable.

June 9, 1539. [MS. Bibliot. Impér. Paris.]

MY LORD,—Parliament, you will see by my letter to the King, is to last till St. John's. The reason, I suppose, is the news from the Levant, and the talked-of council. There is as much excitement about the latter as if it were already a settled thing.

Leave was given to the lords and gentlemen before Whitsuntide to return to their estates; but now the King insists on their remaining in session.

The King's declaration about the sacrament has given wide pleasure and satisfaction. The people in general are inclined to the old religion, and only a few bishops support the new opinions. These bishops are in a bad humour. They wanted leave for the clergy to take wives, and they cannot get it. They desired to make church preferment hereditary, and to convert the benefices into family estates. The gentlemen from Germany did their best to forward the business of priests' marriages, and they are sadly disturbed at their failure. Nor is this their only ground of annoyance. They wanted the King to subsidize them. He refused distinctly, and they now experience what others have found before them, that an Englishman's purse-strings are not easily opened. Thus they are gone off in high dudgeon, and they leave the council equally disgusted with them.

My lord, I need not enlarge on the naval preparations here: there are eighty ships at Portsmouth ready to sail, and

they carry guns of heavier calibre than any hitherto in use at
sea. This may be because the light guns are all exhausted;
there are not half-a-dozen of any kind remaining in the
Tower; seven or eight vessels have been purchased lately from
the Venetians and Florentines, the smallest of which is from
four to five hundred tons; but even in ships so large as these,
the large artillery is dangerous.

So, too, guns are in continual demand for the coast batteries, although for the present year the alarm has passed over.

The King, unlike himself, is in good spirits. For some
years past he has been melancholy, and has avoided society.
Now he forces himself to join in the current amusements.
Every evening he goes on the Thames with musicians and
singers. He takes pleasure in paintings and embroideries; he has
sent to France, Flanders, and Italy for the most accomplished
masters in music and other elegant arts; and those who are
about him think it is a sign that he would marry could he
find a lady to please him.

The Emperor's ambassador is treated with marvellous
civility, and, strange to say, the Queen Regent has allowed the
English agent to buy three thousand harquebusses in Flanders
for the King's service. She has even gone so far as to tell
them, that if they desire they may have as many more. They
are astonished themselves at her condescension.

There has been a funeral service for the late Empress, and
all the great men attended; the two dukes, the lord admiral,
the Lord Cromwell, and other noblemen, with fifteen or
twenty bishops. The mourning will last a fortnight. My
attendance was requested by the King and the Spanish ambassador, so that I could not decline.

Marillac to the Constable.

June 20, 1539.   [MS. Bibliot. Impér. Paris.]

..... For the rest, my lord, may it please you to understand that the day before yesterday there was a grand pastime on the Thames in the King's presence. The affair was
stupid enough. There were two galleys, one of which carried
the royal arms, the other the arms of the Pope, with a number
of cardinals' hats. The galleys encountered and fought a
good while, at last the royal galley had the victory, and Pope,
cardinals, and arms, were all thrown into the water. The
object was to give the people confidence in the King, and to
teach them not to be afraid of the Holy Father and his friends.

K

More and more cannon are founded, and as soon as Parliament rises the King is going on progress two or three hundred miles to survey the works.

Marillac to Francis the First.
July 13, 1539. [MS. Bibliot. Impér. Paris]

SIRE,—The King is all kindness. He speaks in the warmest terms of your Majesty, and I see no trace of unpleasant feeling. So little is he inclined to meddle with your Majesty that he is far more afraid of losing your support; and the dismissal of the musters to their homes is sufficient proof that he has no sinister intentions. The foreign ships are restored to their owners; the ports are opened; the merchants are free to go and come; the dukes and lords who were in London for the Parliament are gone to their own estates; the King is left with scarcely a hundred horse in his train. All these symptoms convince me, Sire, under your correction, that the fleet, the fortresses, and the cannon are merely for defence; and if there were nothing else, the state of feeling about religion is far too critical to allow the King to trifle with the situation. He has been forced to arrest many changes which were in progress before this last Parliament. To satisfy the country, and to silence the Christian Powers, he has restored all the old opinions and constitutions, save the authority of the See of Rome and the orders of monks and nuns; while two bishops who were the chief promoters of the new opinions have been deprived of their sees, and if they will save their lives they must make the best of the time of grace which is allowed them and relinquish their errors. Under these circumstances the King will surely keep on terms with his allies; he will think more of defending the country from attack than of rushing into unprovoked quarrels; and he will never seek a war with one of the strongest countries in the world.

Marillac to the Constable.
July 13, 1539. [MS. Bibliot. Impér. Paris.]

MY LORD,—The King complained in Parliament that the Pope was urging the Emperor and the King of France to attack England on thepretence that the people were heretics and infidels. He said that the belief of the country must be defined, that Christian princes might see the untruth of the Holy Father's accusation.

At the same time, he said, he was ready to meet his Holiness in the field, if necessary, with all his friends. He trusted his subjects would grant him money for the defence of English liberty, and as an example and warning, he demanded justice against those who had plotted treason at home.

England, however, will not seek a quarrel with France. It is true, my lord, that the common people when they had arms in their hands, said, that if the French came over to attack them they would go themselves to France. But these were the vain words of ignorant persons who are our hereditary enemies. To ascertain the King's real views, I spoke the other day to Lord Cromwell about the Anglo-French alliance. He told me, among other strange things, that the Pope and the Emperor had worked hard to incite his master against ours on the ground of the pension: but his Majesty, he said, would not listen to them. As he had begun the subject I went on with it; and said I was told that the King would go to war about the pension, and that Parliament had agreed to it. Lord Cromwell assured me that such a thing had never been so much as thought of.

Marillac to the Constable.

August 12, 1539.   [MS. Bibliot. Impér. Paris.]

My Lord,—I have been more dilatory in writing than you may have expected. The King suddenly left the neighbourhood of London, and came off into Hampshire, sixty miles away.

Being so near Portsmouth and Southampton, I took the opportunity of examining the vessels and works with my own eyes.

Of the fleet lately at Spithead, there remain not more than seven or eight ships in commission, and one large and beautiful galleon. The rest have gone round into the Thames to disembark their armaments. The newly-made fortifications are of great extent, and would serve for a time to protect the place effectively. They are not, however, very durable, having been run up in a hurry, and consisting of double lines of stakes filled in with earth. The King continues his progress, and will return to London to meet Parliament at Michaelmas.

Marillac to Francis the First.

October 25, 1539.   [MS. Bibliot. Impér. Paris.]

SIRE,—I learn from your letter of the 12th, written at Compiegne, that your Majesty wishes to know about the proposed marriage between the King and the sister of the Duke of Cleves.

I have taken the utmost pains to learn the terms of it; but things are kept so secret that for the present I cannot ascertain anything. The King, however, is satisfied, and says openly that he is pleased with the alliance. He will now, he maintains, complete the long-desired league with the Princes of Germany; he will first gain the Duke of Saxe, who has married another sister of the same house; the Duke of Saxe will bring with him the confederation; and the King will find them the means of providing so large an army that no one will venture to meddle with them.

As to religion, his Highness thinks that, with the joint influence of himself and the Duke of Cleves, he can soften down the asperities which are now distracting Germany, and find some honourable middle course by which the troubles there may be composed.

Further, his Highness having but one son, desires to marry for the sake of children, and he considers that he can do no better than take this lady, who is of convenient age, sound health, and fair stature, with many other graces which his Majesty says that she possesses. He has failed to find a wife for himself in France or Spain; and next to your alliance, Sire, or the Emperor's, he considers a connexion with the House of Cleves the best that he can make, especially at this moment, when so many novelties menace the principles of religion, and the German princes show themselves so prompt to defend the doctrines which they were the first to introduce.

News have arrived within the last few days from Flanders, that people there complain that the King ought to have married the Duchess of Milan. The Lady Anne was to have come to England by Calais; but to prevent mischance they talk now of sending for her to the Baltic. Some people say that she will be here in a few days; others, not without show of reason, maintain that she will not be in England till Christmas. Anyhow, they are preparing a splendid reception for her, and in London there will be an especial demonstration, so many advantages are anticipated from the connexion.

Marillac to the Constable.
October 25, 1539. [MS. Bibliot. Impér. Paris.]

MY LORD,—In my letter of the 14th I told you that the new Queen might be looked for very shortly. I have since learnt that she cannot arrive as soon as was expected. We hear from Flanders that the ambassadors of Cleves, who concluded the marriage, returned from Calais to their own country in disguise, and that, since their departure, there has been a great outburst of indignation in Flanders itself. The King, they exclaim, is engaged to the Duchess of Milan, and if he will not keep his word as a man of honour, he shall be compelled to keep it. At all events, they say he shall never have this lady to whom he is now devoting himself.

The report is a strange one, and, in itself, not very credible; but it has troubled those who are easily alarmed, and the council sits at extraordinary hours to devise precautions against accident. So at least I am told. The truth is hard to come at; but they are certainly disturbed about something.

Marillac to the Constable.
December 24, 1539. [MS. Bibliot. Impér. Paris.]

MY LORD,—The new Queen of England arrived at Calais two days ago, and waits a favourable wind to cross. For some time past it has been blowing hard from the westward, and the gale still continues so violent that it is thought she cannot be here for a week at soonest.

Rumour gives the King's eldest daughter to the young Duke of Bavaria, who, as I informed his Majesty, has come over to this country. I see no great likelihood of the truth of the report, except it be that they will probably marry the young lady to a Prince of no great power, for fear of the pretence to the crown, which may be advanced hereafter in her name.

The King is at Greenwich, waiting the arrival of his bride. He proposes to meet her two miles out upon the road; and I and the Emperor's ambassador will be invited, probably, to attend.

Marillac to the Constable.
December 27, 1539. [MS. Bibliot. Impér. Paris.]

MY LORD,—Since I wrote to you on the 24th, I have learnt that the story, the probability of which I doubted, is true. The Lady Mary is really to be married to the Duke of Bavaria. He was taken a few days ago, as secretly as possible, to the gardens at Westminster Abbey. The lady was brought there to meet him, and the Duke gave her a kiss, a thing never done in England by any but near relations unless it means marriage. Since the death of the Marquis of Exeter there has been no man in England of sufficient rank to kiss the Lady Mary.

The Duke talked to her at length, partly in broken German, partly in Latin, which she can speak tolerably well. He told her at last, that the King would let him marry her if she did not find his person displeasing, while she, on her part, replied that her father's pleasure was her own.

When the marriage will come off, I am unable to tell you. People say, however, that it will take place soon; and, from what I hear, I expect it will be in a fortnight, or three weeks at latest. Others think it will be even sooner. The King's nuptials will be celebrated immediately on the lady's arrival, and they say father and daughter will be married on the same day.

Marillac to the Constable.

December 30. [MS. Bibliot. Impér. Paris.]

MY LORD,—M. de Noyon has come to England in disguise. He has been detected; and his presence in such a condition has roused suspicions, in which the Government concur, that his coming has been for something else than amusement. The season of the year, so unsuited for travelling, the rank of the person, whom they know to be both a bishop and a peer of France, with the few servants who were found in his company, have combined to persuade them that he had some secret practice in hand either in Scotland, or with the Church party in England.

Had I not used my best skill and played them a trick their misgivings would not have been easily removed. I took care, however, neither to see the bishop nor to speak with him till he had been with the King, that they might not think I had put his story into his mouth; and in this way I have satisfied them that he came over on his own account merely. To stop the world's mouth, I have insisted that he shall immediately return, and he has made no difficulty. He is as disgusted at having been discovered, as I am at his having come at all. People were never in a more suspicious humour than at this moment.

The affair has turned out better than might have been expected. The King was gracious enough, and talked pleasantly to him about the King his brother. This, however, does not prevent others from using their tongues, and talking spitefully of the French.

Marillac to Francis the First.

Jan. 5, 1540. [MS. Bibliot. Impér. Paris.]

SIRE,—On Friday, the second of this month, notice was given by the public crier that the Lady Anne of Cleves was coming to Greenwich, and that the King's liege subjects were expected to be present to receive her. I and the Emperor's ambassador had an invitation in the King's name; and the concourse of people, which was large and imposing, went off without disorder or confusion. Five or six thousand horse, with the Dukes of Norfolk and Suffolk, were in attendance on the lady. The King and his household, and five thousand more, rode out from Greenwich to meet her.

She was in a Flemish costume. The King received her with all politeness, and conducted her to the palace, where a splendid suite of rooms was prepared for her. Her age one would guess at about thirty. She is tall and thin, and not particularly pretty. Her countenance shows assurance and resolution. She has twelve or fifteen ladies with her, all dressed as strangely as herself; and in her train is the ambassador of Saxe also, who, people say, is come to conclude the so-often-commenced treaty between his master and the King. Henceforward they say the King and the German league are to be at one, and will share each other's fortunes for good and ill. The truth will be known in the next Parliament, which meets in Lent. A round sum of money has to be demanded; and the King supposes, and the council say, that he may have a million crowns without distressing his subjects.

Marillac to the Constable.

Jan. 5, 1540. [MS. Bibliot. Impér. Paris.]

. . . . . . People who have seen the lady close say that she is neither as young as was expected, nor as pretty as she was reported to be. She is tall, and her face and carriage have a force in them which shows she is not without mind. The spirit and sense will perhaps supply the deficiency of beauty.

The twelve or fifteen ladies she has brought with her are even less good-looking than their mistress; and they are dressed so hideously that, if they were beauties, they would look detestable.

The King met her at the bottom of the hill, two miles from Greenwich. Including her own retinue, she had five or six thousand horse with her. I would describe the procession, had you not yourself seen many such here. The English wore no ornaments but massive gold chains; and for general splendour there were twenty scenes more striking in France during the late passage of the Emperor.*

Marillac to Francis the First.

Jan. 28, 1540.   [MS. Bibliot. Impér. Paris.]

SIRE,—The German ambassadors went a week ago. Duke Philip of Bavaria, after being made a Knight of the Garter, started yesterday with a present of five or six thousand crowns from the King. His marriage, I am told, is finally settled, and he will return shortly.

They were in a panic here while the Emperor was in France. Since he went they have recovered their spirits. The German league is perhaps succeeding to their satisfaction, or they are on better terms with the Emperor again. I shall know more in a few days.

Marillac to the Constable.

Feb. 2, 1540.   [MS. Bibliot. Impér. Paris.]

MY LORD,—My cousin will have informed you of the general course of events here. As to the league between France and England, the council have more than once felt their way towards it with me, and the King himself touched the subject in a word or two. There is nothing they are more anxious about than to remain on good terms with us. They know the advantage which they derive from our King's support,

---

* In December and January, 1539-1540, Charles V. crossed France from Spain to the Low Countries. His reception at Paris was supposed to have a political meaning most unfavourable to England.

and the injury which they might sustain if they lost it. Their public policy had two mainstays, and both have failed them. They anticipate the utmost mischief from the good understanding between our master and the Emperor, and their alarm is increased by the report that peace is probable between the Emperor, the Turks, and the Venetians. They expected our master, the Turks, and the Emperor, to be so busy with one another, as to have no leisure to meddle with them; and now, unless there be truth in the rumour that the Emperor means to recover Gueldres, they consider themselves quite certain to be attacked.

If the Gueldres affair goes forward, they will perhaps subsidize the Duke of Cleves and the princes of the League, so as to divert the war from this country, and keep it as far distant from them as possible, till they can make terms with the Emperor, and settle their own concerns.

At the same time, my lord, I am sure that they will court France as long as they know the Emperor to be ill disposed towards them. And when they talk to me of the King's friendship, if I do my master no good by listening graciously to them, at least I am doing no harm.

Marillac to Francis the First.
Feb. 16, 1540. [MS. Bibliot. Impér. Paris.]

SIRE,—I informed the King of the indecent and insolent behaviour of the English ambassador, and I requested his Highness on your behalf, and in the words which you were pleased to command, to recall the said ambassador at his earliest convenience, and to send some one in his place who would discharge the office more properly. The King and council were most courteous. After many gracious expressions of regret, the King promised, as a proof of his desire to preserve your Majesty's friendship, that an order should be sent to the ambassador, by the bearer of this present letter, commanding him to return immediately. Sir John Wallop, the Governor of Calais, will receive instructions to take his place.

His Highness, however, while consenting to the recall, desired that I would ask your Majesty to show some tokens of forgiveness to the said ambassador; and when he should present himself to take leave, he hoped you would speak less harshly to him than his fault had merited. He said he would gladly spare an old servant, who had done good work in times past, and might do good work again when better instructed in his duty, the ignominy of a public dismissal. The ambassador holds a high office in the Church also, being Bishop of the Metropolitan See of London.

Marillac to the Constable.

March 7, 1540. [MS. Bibliot. Impér. Paris.]

MY LORD,—In default of matters of greater importance, I may tell you of an occurrence of which more may be heard hereafter.

A controversy about religion has broken out between the Bishop of Winchester, and the late ambassador in France the Bishop of London, on one side, and on the other a doctor named Barnes, a noted preacher of German opinions. The dispute began thus:—On a Sunday at the beginning of Lent, the Bishop of Winchester preached a sermon at Paul's Cross, in which he discussed and refuted these opinions like a man of learning. This Doctor Barnes was unable to endure. A few days after, although it was not his turn to preach, he found means to take the place of the proper person, and from the same pulpit contradicted what the bishop had said. He spoke with much heat and ill temper; and, at length, he flung his glove among the crowd in defiance of his adversary, saying, he would maintain his doctrines against him to the death.

The King, when informed of what had passed, was much troubled and scandalized. His Highness and council will sit as judges, and the bishop and doctor are to dispute before them. They are to produce their sermons in writing, and whichever is proved to be in the wrong will be punished as his offence shall deserve.

Marillac to the Constable.

March 26, 1540. [MS. Bibliot. Impér. Paris.]

MY LORD,—Nothing worth noticing has happened since my last letter. They seem chiefly anxious to avoid war, and to be on good terms with France.

Lord Cromwell says that the differences between the Emperor and the Duke of Cleves are on the point of arrangement. He perhaps likes to think so. Englishmen are always glad of excuses to escape finding their friends in money.

The appointment of the Pope's nephew as legate at the Imperial Court is talked of. It is thought he will bring the excommunication with him, and try again to form a coalition against England.

They protest that in all points but the Papal supremacy and the religious orders, their creed is identical with ours; but they think the Turks will leave Christian Powers no leisure to make war on one another, and they feel little anxiety.

They talk of the approach of their usual season of amusements after Easter. The Queen's coronation will be at Whitsuntide.

Marillac to Francis the First.

April 10, 1540. [MS. Bibliot. Impér. Paris.]

SIRE,—Since the return of the Duke of Norfolk from France, nothing of moment has happened here. The King only gives constant proofs of his desire to be on good terms with your Majesty.

He is not exactly afraid that you will desert him; yet his confidence is not so strong but that he has moments of misgiving. He dreads to lose your support, from the greatness of his anxiety to retain it.

For other matters, Sire, you may remember that last year there was an Act of Parliament bringing religion into conformity with Catholic doctrine. The See of Rome and the institution of monks were the sole points on which differences were left remaining; and as to the monks, there is not one in all England who is not now dressed as a secular priest. But in matters of doctrine the orders then taken have been ill observed. The statute has been infringed by the Anabaptists and the Germanizers. There have been outbreaks in Calais and Southampton, and, in defiance of the King's injunctions, meat has been eaten in Lent, and sermons openly preached against abstinence.

Commissioners have gone to the two towns to punish the rioters, and since Easter three doctors have been committed to the Tower as the authors of the new opinions. Of these, the most considerable is Doctor Barnes, who has lately returned from Germany, and has published more than one heretical book.

The same Doctor Barnes (it shows what a fool the man is) possessed himself irregularly one day in Lent of the pulpit at St. Paul's, and broke into outrageous abuse of the Bishop of Winchester, who had preached there the Sunday before. Such a proceeding was likely to lead to a breach of the peace. The King, therefore, sharply reprimanded the doctor, sent him to beg the bishop's pardon, and ordered him afterwards to preach another sermon, withdrawing his errors, and apologizing for his conduct. He obeyed, but in a manner which showed he was acting merely in constrained obedience to the King. He is therefore now in the Tower, with two of his accomplices; and ten or twelve London citizens and fifteen or twenty foreigners have been arrested with him. The latter are chiefly Flemish Anabaptists.

The trials will soon come forward—in the next session of Parliament at latest, which begins the 20th of this month.

There will be a fresh Act of Religion. This subject fills all men's minds, and nothing else is talked of, unless it be the return of the Duke of Bavaria to complete his marriage with the Lady Mary, and the intended jousts at the Queen's coronation.

Marillac to the Constable.

April 14, 1540. [MS. Bibliot. Impér. Paris.]

. . . . . Duke Philip is soon looked for. I am assured more positively than ever that the marriage is to come off. The Duke is to have but 40,000 crowns with the Lady Mary, or 9000*l*. sterling—payable, too, in three years. Moreover, she is held illegitimate.

You are perhaps aware that the wife of the late marquis who was beheaded has been liberated from the Tower. Her son remains there, and the nephew and mother of Cardinal Pole. The latter, however, will, it is said, be soon released; the boys will most likely remain where they are, to prevent trouble to the succession.

Marillac to the Constable.

April 24, 1540. [MS. Bibliot. Impér. Paris.]

. . . . . I have this important news for you since I last wrote. The Lord Cromwell has been appointed Earl of Essex and Grand Chamberlain of England. He is now in as high favour with his master as ever he was; but he has been nearly shaken from his place by the Bishop of Winchester and the rest.

Four hundred harquebuss men have been levied for Ireland. The majority of those who were sent last year have been killed by the insurgents.

Marillac to the Constable.

May 8, 1540. [MS. Bibliot. Impér. Paris.]

MY LORD,—From my conversation with the King and his ministers, I should gather that each of them have a part allotted them to play one after the other.

Lord Cromwell, to whom I went on some police business, began with telling me of the singular affection of his master for the most Christian King. He said that, like others, he had once been more Imperialist than French; but he had ascertained that the Emperor, while he amused the world with fair words, was designing, when opportunity offered, to make himself sole monarch of Christendom. He had opened his eyes, and English statesmen, he said, thought now only of extinguishing a fire which else would burn up the world,

The day after the King spoke to me . . . . . . His language was far more sober, and without the passion of his ministers. Either he thought moderation more dignified, or he has more prudence in keeping his thoughts to himself.

After him the Duke of Norfolk took up the tale respecting what had been said by Lord Cromwell, and the Duke of Suffolk and the rest followed in the same strain.

Marillac to the Constable.

May 21, 1540. [MS. Bibliot. Impér. Paris.]

MY LORD,—I was with the King a few days since at Greenwich. I had to attend divine service there, as usual, at Whitsuntide, and I wanted information on a variety of matters of which I am about to speak.

The Parliament, my lord, was to have ended before the holidays. The work was done. The King's subsidy was granted—two shillings in the pound, payable in three years. The Knights of St. John are to surrender their white crosses. Their lands go to the crown; and the two grants together will yield, it is expected, above three million crowns. All, in short, which was demanded had been acceded to without opposition, and the Houses would have broken up had it not been for difficulties with religion where the bishops have been unable to come to an agreement. In the way they go on they would make things worse rather than better, were it not that the King keeps them in some sort of order. He hears their arguments and listens to their opinions; but the determination will be with himself; and the ministers assure me that a book will soon appear, with the sanction of Parliament, where every man may learn what he is to believe, and doubtful points will be decided neither by German views nor Papal views, but by the authority of the early Christian Church.

The Duke of Saxe and the league have lately sent over the articles on which they have themselves agreed, and they expect to see them accepted in England; but I feel pretty sure that they will find themselves mistaken. People say the articles are full of heresies.

My lord, the day before yesterday, at ten o'clock at night, the Deputy of Calais, the King's uncle, was brought prisoner to the Tower. To-day one of his chaplains has been arrested also. I do not know the reason. The world say the deputy was in correspondence with Cardinal Pole, and that there was some practice for the betrayal of Calais. Ten or twelve Calais pensioners are charged with having spoken treasonable words; and I learn from a credible quarter that a great personage, I know not who, is about to be arrested also. Anything passes for high treason here now. Men are laid hold of day after day for the most opposite reasons. A person named Lee, who has been ten or twelve years abroad, is in the Tower for having communicated with Pole. Others have been seized for eating meat in Lent—others for not observing Easter. They are busy with their fleet again. Twenty or thirty ships are gone to the coast of Scotland to watch the movements of the French, who are said to be in communication with the Irish rebels.

Marillac to Francis the First.

June 1, 1540. [MS. Bibliot. Impér. Paris.]

SIRE,—Since the Deputy of Calais was brought over prisoner, two other men—men of some note—from the same town, have been sent for, and are in the Tower. The Bishop of Chichester and the Dean of the Chapel Royal, whom your Majesty may remember as ambassador at your Court, have been arrested on a charge of high treason; and with them one of the King's chaplains, a man of reputation for learning. This last is said to have been in correspondence with Rome in the times of the late marquis. The rest of the bishops are in terror. They are afraid that they also may be made out guilty; and their fate will be certain. The religious strife has become so bitter that each party will destroy their antagonists if they can. There will be prisoners enough between them by and by; and when Parliament will now end, it is impossible to say.

Marillac to the Constable.

June 1, 1540. [MS. Bibliot. Impér. Paris.]

My Lord,—A few days since the Dean of the Chapel Royal and the Bishop of Chichester were conducting the service in state at Westminster Abbey, when they were arrested, and sent to the Tower for treason, and before night their goods were seized and confiscated.

Lord Cromwell, I hear from a credible quarter, says that other bishops are about to follow. I did not learn their names, but we may presume them to be those who lately shook Cromwell's credit, and brought him nearly to his ruin. However that be, things are now at a pass when either Cromwell's party or the Bishop of Winchester's party must fall; and although they are both high in favour and authority with the King their master, fortune will most probably turn in favour of Cromwell. The Dean of the Chapel, the Bishop of Winchester's best friend, is struck down; the Archbishop of Canterbury, his greatest adversary, has been deputed to preach in the bishop's place at St. Paul's, and has begun to argue against his doctrines in the same pulpit where the bishop preached in Lent. Doctor Barnes, who was lately imprisoned, is likely to be soon released at the intercession of the Germans; and another doctor, named Latimer, who last year surrendered his see rather than subscribe to the Six Articles, is recalled, and will shortly be replaced upon the bench.

So great is the inconstancy here, and so lightly opinion changes.

The state of religion continues most unfortunate. The bishops are divided, and hate one another. The people know not what to believe; for those who are inclined to the reformed views are called heretics; those who adhere to the old faith are charged with Papistry and treason. They ought to dissolve Parliament, and find some middle way for the country to follow. But as far as I can see, it will be as with the Diets in Germany, and the confusion, instead of being pacified, will grow worse and worse.

Marillac to Francis the First.

June 10, 1540. [MS. Bibliot. Impér. Paris.]

SIRE,—I am this moment informed that Mr. Thomas Cromwell,* Keeper of the Privy Seal, and the King's Vicar-General in matters spiritual, who since the death of the cardinal has had the chief conduct of the affairs of this realm, and was lately made Grand Chamberlain of England, has, within an hour, been sent prisoner to the Tower, and his goods are in the hands of justice.

This news need not have been of especial consequence. Such persons are often reduced to the rank out of which they have been raised, and are treated as every one declares this man has deserved to be treated. Cromwell, however, has been the chief author of all the innovations in religion; and in the present state of affairs, and from the probability that there will now be a change, his downfall is so important that it is my duty to inform you of it immediately. At this time I can say no more. The doctrinal questions are still unsettled, and the bishops as far from a conclusion as ever.

Sire, as I was about to close my letter, there came a gentleman of the Court to me with a message from the King. His Highness desires me not to be alarmed by the arrest of Lord Cromwell; and because the common people talk wildly and ignorantly, and that I may have something better than conjecture to send to your Majesty, he wishes me to learn the exact truth from himself.

The substance of his explanation is this. The King has endeavoured, by all the means in his power, to compose the religious differences in this realm. Cromwell has lent himself to the Lutherans, and has abused his authority to show favour to the teachers of false opinions, and to oppress and hinder their opponents.

Being admonished of late by some of his servants that he was acting contrary to his master's wishes and to the statutes of the realm, he betrayed himself, and revealed his secret intentions. He said that he hoped to put down alto-

---

* The reader will observe the change in Cromwell's designation.

gether the old preachers, and leave none but the new; that in brief time he would bring things to such a pass, that the King, with all his power, should not be able to hinder him; and that his party would be so strong, that whether the King would or no, the King should accept the new doctrines, if he had himself to take arms and fight for them. The victory in the struggle would be with him, and thus he would establish at last the views for which he had long contended.

The persons to whom Cromwell said these words revealed them to the King, more regarding their duties than the favour of their own master.

His Majesty says also that the first time he is in conversasion with me he will tell me other things which will prove how deep Lord Cromwell's fault has been.

Marillac to the Constable..

June 10, 1540.   [MS. Bibliot. Impér. Paris.]

MY LORD,—I explained to you in my last letter the divisions of the Privy Council, how one part was trying to destroy the other. Lord Cromwell's party appeared the strongest; a few days since he was able to arrest the Dean of the Chapel and the Bishop of Chichester. But the party have now fallen in the fall of Lord Cromwell himself; there remain of them only the Archbishop of Canterbury, whose mouth for the future will be closed, and the lord admiral, who has long learnt to trim his sails to the wind. Against them are the Duke of Norfolk and all the rest.

It is indeed a marvellous change, and passes expectation.

Francis the First to Marillac.

June 15, 1540.   [MS. Bibliot. Impér. Paris.]

M. MARILLAC,—Sir John Wallop, the minister of my good brother the King of England, has this day informed me, on the part of my said brother, of the arrest of Mr. Cromwell.

The news is more than grateful to me. It is such as I give most hearty thanks for to Almighty God, who has been my brother's perpetual friend and support.

You will lay my letter to yourself before the King. I send

L

a duplicate for the purpose. You will tell him from me that he has occasion to show himself grateful to the Almighty, who has thus revealed to him the crimes and misdoings of this unhappy man.

It was this Cromwell who was the cause of the suspicions which my good brother has entertained against his most faithful subjects. God has made the truth to be known, and now, when my good brother has removed the wicked wretch from his councils, he will perceive what God has done for the tranquillity of the realm, and the common welfare of nobles and people.

For the regard I bear him, M. Marillac, I feel myself obliged to dwell on this thing. I entreat him to take my words in good part as proceeding from a sincere and honest good-will towards him. My cousin, the Duke of Norfolk, will remember my language when he was last at this Court. I would have you show him this letter before you communicate it to the King.

M. Marillac, I pray God have you in his keeping.

Written at Fontainebleau, June 15, 1540.

Marillac to the Constable.

June 23, 1540. [MS. Bibliot. Impér. Paris.]

MY LORD,—There is nothing to tell you except what concerns Lord Cromwell; all other business is cast aside that they may attend exclusively to him; and they are so swift in their operations that it is thought in a week, at latest, he will die the traitor's death that he has deserved.

The arrest took place in the council chamber at the Palace at Westminster. The Lieutenant of the Tower entered with the King's commands to take him prisoner. In a burst of passion he clutched his cap and flung it on the ground. 'This, then,' he said to the Duke of Norfolk and the rest of the council assembled there, 'this, then, is my guerdon for the service that I have done. On your consciences, I ask you, am I a traitor? I may have offended, but never with my will. Such faults as I have committed deserve grace and pardon; but if the King my master believes so ill of me, let him make quick work and not leave me to languish in prison.'

Part of the council exclaimed that he was a traitor; part said he should be judged by the bloody laws which he had himself made; words idly spoken he had twisted into treason; the measure which he had dealt to others should now be meted out to him.

The Duke of Norfolk, after reproaching him with his many villanies, tore the St. George from his neck. The admiral,* to show that he was as much his enemy in adversity as in prosperity he had pretended to be his friend, stripped off the Garter. He was then led down into a barge by a gate which opened on the river, and was conducted to the Tower. The people in the City knew nothing of his arrest until they saw Mr. Cheyne and two archers of the guards at his house door.

His effects appear by the inventory to be of less value than was expected : though enough, and too much, for so base a fellow. He had £7,000 sterling in silver money. The silver vessels, crosses, chalices, mitres, goblets, and other spoils of the Church, might amount to rather more. The whole was carried in the night to the royal treasury, a sign that there was no intention of restoring it.

The following morning many letters were found—letters which he had himself written to the Germans; others which he had received from them. I do not know the contents; but the King is so exasperated that he will not hear him speak, and is only anxious to put away the very memory of him as of the vilest wretch that ever was born in the realm. His offices will be bestowed as you will see below; and the public criers have gone through the City, proclaiming that he is not to be called Lord Privy Seal or by any other title of honour, but solely Master Thomas Cromwell. His privileges and prerogatives of nobility are taken from him. The less valuable of his effects are distributed among his servants, who are forbidden to wear their master's livery, and it is thought he will not be admitted to trial as a peer of the realm,† or be executed with a peer's privilege by the axe. He will be hanged like any common villain.

The fate of the other prisoners in the Tower is uncertain. There are hopes for the Deputy of Calais. The King said a few days ago, he could not find that the deputy had erred through malice. His faults had arisen more from ignorance than any other cause.

My lord, it remains to tell you who have succeeded to Cromwell's offices. The admiral becomes Privy Seal. Lord Russell goes to the Admiralty. The Bishop of Durham is

---

* Fitzwilliam, Earl of Southampton.
† This is, perhaps, the explanation of the process against Cromwell being by attainder. The lords would not acknowledge him as their peer.

Chief Secretary. About the Vicar-generalship of the spiritualty no resolution is yet taken. If they appoint any one, it will be the Bishop of Winchester, who since the fall of his great adversary has returned to the Privy Council.

Judicial matters will be managed by the chancellor, who, in addition to his other merits, speaks neither French nor Latin, and is a most accomplished seller of justice whenever he can find a merchant to buy it. His colleague is the Chancellor of Augmentations,* the worst man in all England; the first inventor of the dissolution of the abbeys, and of all subsequent changes. The Chancellor of Augmentations invented, Cromwell furnished the authority. He held his office for the increase of the revenue of the crown; but for all that he might be more fitly called the ' Chancellor of Diminutions.' He is able and learned, but he uses his talents only for evil.

Marillac to Francis the First.

July 6, 1540. [MS. Bibliot. Impér. Paris.]

SIRE,—The Parliament will last till the end of this month; when it is over we shall see how things will be. For the present I have nothing to write, unless it be that the King tells me he means to grant a general pardon of all crimes and offences committed by his subjects, those persons only being excepted from the benefit of it who are attainted by Act of Parliament for high treason. Among these last is Cromwell, who will be executed, the Duke of Norfolk desires me to tell you, as soon as ever Parliament rises. The mode of his death, the duke says, will be the most ignominious which is practised n this country.

Marillac to the Constable.

July 6, 1540. [MS. Bibliot. Impér. Paris.]

MY LORD,—I have received the letters which his Majesty and your lordship were pleased to write to me, dated the 28th of last month, and have seen by the enclosure the account of the conversation which the Most Christian King held with the Pope's ambassador. I see nothing in this to cause surprise. This King has often used the same language to myself. As to the Pope and the Emperor, you know, my lord, he not

---

* Sir R. Ryche, afterwards Lord Ryche.

only calls his Holiness mere Bishop of Rome—which is the
title by which his Holiness is now uniformly designated here
—but he heaps upon him contumelious expressions, calling
him abomination, child of perdition, an idol, and an Antichrist; and as to the Emperor, I never speak to his Majesty
but what he uses much the same words of him also. On the
other hand, when talking of France, he never once makes
mention either of pension or tribute; he never complains of
the fortifications of Ardes, or of any other thing, unless it be
that we are holding off from him, and preferring others to him,
who will never be our sincere friends.

As to other things ; you will have understood by my
cyphered letter of the first of this month, that there was some
diminution of regard towards the Queen on the King's part,
and a disposition toward another woman. The Queen has
been sent to Richmond. The King promised to follow her
two days later; but I know for certain that he has not been
there, nor does he talk of going. The route which he has
appointed for his progress does not approach that neighbourhood. It is said in the Court that she has withdrawn to be
out of danger of the plague, which they pretend has appeared in the City. But that is false. There are no signs of
the plague. If there were, the King would not stay for the
most important business in the world. I do not know a man
so timid in such cases as he.

Marillac to Francis the First.

July 8, 1540. [MS. Bibliot. Impér. Paris.]

SIRE,—I had a message from the King yesterday morning,
requiring my presence at the Court. The Emperor's ambassador had a similar invitation, and on our appearance we were
conducted into the council chamber, neither of us knowing
why we were sent for.

The Privy Council were assembled, and the Bishop of Durham then addressed us in Latin. He said that the clergy, and
the lords and commons assembled in Parliament, had ascertained
that there were certain hindrances to the marriage celebrated
five months previously between his Majesty and the sister of
the Duke of Cleves; and that no disputes might hereafter arise
touching the inheritance to the crown, they had entreated his
Majesty, for his own welfare and for theirs, to allow the said
hindrances to be examined by Parliament, in order that the

question whether the marriage was or was not valid might receive a conclusive answer.

To this request the King had been pleased to consent, and his Majesty had desired that we should be informed of what had taken place, that we might send a true account to our respective Courts, and not be at the mercy of rumour.

To this harangue I replied, that for my part I never ventured to speak of Kings without due discretion, and in a matter of such importance I should not dream of writing without accurate knowledge; the honour of Sovereigns required to be treated with more reverence. Nevertheless, I said, I thanked the King much for having thus openly informed me of the truth, and I would transmit it faithfully, as my master's service required. I added, that if they desired I would furnish them with a copy of my letter; but this they graciously refused. They were satisfied, they said, that I should write nothing but the truth; and I then returned to my lodgings. The courier should have set out immediately, but the passages have remained for two days closed. They were afraid, I suppose, of the story transpiring through an unauthorized channel.

Marillac to Francis the First.

July 21, 1540. [MS. Bibliot. Impér. Paris.]

SIRE,—The marriage between the King and the Lady Anne of Cleves is still under discussion, and things have gone so far that by the joint sentence of all the bishops in England, and with the sanction of Parliament, the said marriage is declared null and at an end. The King has sworn in the presence of the council, that the Lady Anne has never been more than formally his wife, that the marriage had not been consummated, and that the consent required to give it efficacy was wanting from the first. It is also declared that she was before engaged to the son of the Duke of Lorraine, and that the King, having entered into the contract in ignorance of those conditions, is not bound to it.

The lady being asked if she would accept the bishops for her judges, assented willingly. The Duke her brother's ambassador urged her again and again, as he himself assured me, to consent to nothing; but she declared that she would do only what would please the King her lord; she had received nothing but kindness from him, and she would submit to anything that he thought proper. If he wished it, she would remain in the realm and not return to her own country.

In return for the lady's readiness, the King has settled upon her an honourable maintenance. He has given her either Richmond Palace or Moor Park for her life. She may take which she will, with twelve thousand crowns a year.

No one, however, is to call her Queen any more, but simply the Lady Anne of Cleves, to the great regret of the people, who esteemed and loved her as the most gentle and gracious princess that they had ever known.

For the rest, Sire, it is said generally that the King is going to marry a lady of great beauty, daughter of a brother of the Duke of Norfolk. Indeed, if I were to report a scandal which I have heard from more quarters than one, the marriage has already taken place. I cannot certainly say, however, that this is so. I shall know more in a few days.

Parliament concludes to-morrow. The Act on Religion will be in unison with the teaching of the Church; and the separation from Rome and the suppression of the monks will remain the sole points of discrepancy. Another thing, strange enough, has been resolved on. All foreigners residing in this realm are required to leave it before Michaelmas, excepting such as are engaged in trade; and of those who are so engaged, none may be householders unless they are married, or unless they have letters granted them of nationality.

A number of poor creatures are in consternation at this order, especially Flemings, who are here in large numbers.

Marillac to the Constable.

July 29, 1540. [MS. Bibliot. Impér. Paris.]

MY LORD,—Master Thomas Cromwell was beheaded this morning at the usual place. Grace was shown him in the fashion of his death, which was to have been more ignominious.

With him suffered also the Lord Hungerford, a man about forty years old, who had committed sodomy, had violated his daughter, had practised magic, and dealt with the devil.

There will be more executions this week. There are several persons condemned by Act of Parliament, and not comprehended in the general pardon, who lie at the King's mercy, either to die or to remain in prison for their lives.

Marillac to Francis the First.

August 6, 1540. [MS. Bibliot. Impér. Paris.]

SIRE,—You will have heard of the execution of Master Cromwell and Lord Hungerford. Two days after, six more were put to death; three were hanged as traitors, Fetherstone, Abel, and Cook, late Prior of Doncaster, for having spoken in favour of the Pope; three were burnt as heretics, Garret, Jerome, and Doctor Barnes. It was a strange spectacle to see the adherents of two opposite parties die thus on the same day and at the same hour, and it was equally disgraceful to the two divisions of the Government who pretended to have received offence. The scene was as painful as it was monstrous. Both groups of sufferers were obstinate or constant: both alike complained of the mode of sentence under which they were condemned. They had never been called to answer for their supposed offences; and Christians under grace, they said, were now worse off than Jews under the law. The law would have no man die unless he were first heard in his defence, and Heathen and Christian, sage and emperor, the whole world, except England, observed the same rule.

Here in England, if two witnesses will swear and affirm before the council that they have heard a man speak against his duty to his King, or contrary to the articles of religion, that man may be condemned to suffer death, with the pains appointed by the law, although he be absent or ignorant of the charge, and without any other form of proof. Innocence is no safeguard when such an opening is offered to malice or revenge. Corruption or passion may breed false witness; and the good may be sacrificed, and the wicked, who have sworn away their lives, may escape with impunity. There is no security for any man, unless the person accused is brought face to face with the witnesses who depose against him.

Of the iniquity of the system no other evidence is needed than these executions just passed. One who suffered for treason declared that he had never spoken good or bad of the Pope's authority, nor could he tell how he had provoked the King's displeasure, unless it were, that ten years ago his opinion was required on the divorce of Queen Catherine, the Emperor's aunt, and he had said he considered her the King's lawful wife. The rest spoke equally firmly and equally simply, and such loud murmurs rose among the people, and their natural disposition to turbulence was so excited, that had there been any one to lead them, they would have broken out into dangerous sedition. Inquiries were made instantly into the origin of the riot. The names of those who have repeated the words of the sufferers have been demanded, and this, I suppose, will be made the occasion of a worse butchery. It is no easy thing to keep a people in revolt against the Holy See and the authority of the Church, and yet free from the infection of the new doctrines—or, on the other hand, if they remain orthodox, to prevent them from looking with attachment to the Papacy. But the council here will have neither the one nor the other. They will have their ordinances obeyed, however often they change them, and however little the people can comprehend what they are required to believe.

The King is ten miles off at Hampton Court, thinly attended, and has been lately at Richmond to visit the Queen that was. He is on the best possible terms with her, and they supped so pleasantly together that some thought she was to be restored to her place. Others say, however, that the King merely wanted to tell her what had been done, and required her signature to the deed of separation; and this is most likely the true account of the thing, for three of the Privy Council were brought in, who are not in general admitted to such terms of familiarity. It would argue too great inconstancy, it would reflect too much on the King's honour, to put her away on a plea of conscience and take her back so easily. If she might justly be his wife, why did he put her away so precipitately? If there were lawful impediments to the marriage, by what right could he take her back? Moreover, she was not treated with as much distinction as when Queen. She had then a seat at his side. On this occasion she sat at a little distance at a table joining the corner of the table where the King sat.

However, I will write more fully when I can obtain certain intelligence.

Marillac to the Constable.

August 15, 1540.   [MS. Bibliot. Impér. Paris.]

MY LORD,—The King, with a small retinue, is gone to the chase, and the nobility are scattered to their homes. Till now there has been some uncertainty about the new Queen who has succeeded the Duke of Cleves' sister; but this morning she was prayed for in the churches in the usual form, with the King and the Prince.

The Lady of Cleves, so far from being troubled at what has befallen her, appears as happy as ever she was in her life. Every day she comes out in a new dress of some strange fashion or other, and either she is preternaturally prudent in concealing her feelings, or, considering how much her honour has been touched, she is utterly stupid and insensible.

However that be, the ambassador of Cleves has fretted himself into a fever. He begs me every day to let him know what I hear about his master, and what is said about the new marriage.

Marillac to Francis the First.

September 3, 1540. [MS. Bibliot. Impér. Paris.]

SIRE,—I have already informed your Majesty of the nuptials of the new Queen, the niece of the Duke of Norfolk, who has been substituted for the lady now called only my Lady of Cleves.

The latter, so far from being miserable at her treatment, betrays in her face no signs of dissatisfaction whatever, and amuses herself in all possible ways with dresses and entertainments.

Out hunting the other day, the King talked to me with much graciousness, and spoke at length of his regard for your Majesty. Among other things, he bade me tell you that the time was approaching when you would find the truth of what he had always predicted—meaning, the reopening of the quarrel between your Majesty and the Emperor.

The Emperor, he said, had for some days past been endeavouring to draw him over to his side; but experience of the past had made him wary; he had received many fine words from the Emperor, but the words had flown away, and no effect had followed.

Marillac to the Constable.

September 3, 1540. [MS. Bibliot. Impér. Paris.]

MY LORD,—I have nothing particular to write to you, except that during this progress I have seen the new Queen. Her beauty is nothing particular, and she is very small and slight; but she is remarkably graceful; her countenance is modest, soft, and gentle; and the King is so fond of her that he knows not how to express his affection. She dresses in French fashion like the other ladies of the Court, and she reigns supreme. The Lady of Cleves, meanwhile, shows herself perfectly happy. Her brother's ambassador tells me she is in the best spirits in the world.

In November an embassy was sent to the Emperor, and Marillac was instructed to find out the object of it.

Marillac to Francis the First.

November 16. [MS. Bibliot. Impér. Paris.]

SIRE,—I have no certainty to tell you. Nevertheless, it may be to the purpose to give you generally the results of the many opinions expressed about this embassy.

The first possibility is, that the King may desire to clear his conduct to the Emperor and the German princes in divorcing the Duke of Cleves' sister and in marrying his present Queen.

Secondly, he may wish to explain the order which he has introduced in religion; the council pretending that they have established nothing which is not in conformity with the apostolic constitutions and the doctrines of the primitive church.

The King probably knows that on these two points the Germans are offended and scandalized. The majority have renounced the friendship which they had commenced with him, and when occasion serves, they will show their resentment to the extent of their power. It is probable, also, that in their Diets and assemblies they will give some marked proof of the indignation which they have conceived against the King. They will be able to allege that he has never observed the marriage law, except so far as has suited his inclination; and that in religion the English have done nothing except to gratify their ambition and avarice.

To reply to these and similar charges, it is thought that the King has despatched the Bishop of Winchester, who was the chief adviser of this last marriage, by which he worked the ruin of the late Lord Cromwell; while the bishop also, being a man of some knowledge, may explain how, in religion, things are restored unto their original condition, and by the number of his retinue may show that the Church of England is neither so impoverished nor despoiled as the world has thought.

These views, Sire, have appearance of reason in them, and have been suggested to me by persons who have means of knowing what they speak of. For myself, were I permitted to guess with the rest, I should think the King's chief motive was to practise with the Emperor through this embassy, as he practised with you, Sire, through the Duke of Norfolk. The English know that they have offended all the world, and therefore they distrust all the world. They fear that the princes of Christendom may one day unite to punish them, and they can find no better security for themselves than in the differences which they can excite between the two chief States of Christendom. They suppose that when these two heads move, all the members must move with them, and that when you are in discord you will have no leisure to interfere with them.

The fortifications are continued throughout the island wherever an enemy can land. A German engineer, who has designed the ramparts at Guisnes and Calais, has been brought over to plan some other works at home.

The Duke of Suffolk, I am told, is going in three or four days to Calais to inspect. Some say he will go further; but it is unlikely. He is not of an age to undertake a long journey.

The King, with a few servants only, has been for two days in London, as it were incognito. He wanted to see certain machines of war, and contrivances for throwing fire, invented by his German and Italian workmen. His Majesty has lately fitted out six light galleys, which he has armed and equipped like your Highness's at Marseilles. They will go to sea before next Easter, and they are to ply between Calais and this coast, where they will make the passage with more certainty than sailing vessels.

Marillac to the Constable.

November 16, 1540. [MS. Bibliot. Impér. Paris.]

MY LORD,— I have written so fully to the King that I think I have nothing to add, unless it be touching the mission of the Bishop of Winchester, which some think is to arrange a marriage between the Lady Mary and the Emperor. I cannot but believe such a match to be out of the question. In the first place, by all Estates of the Realm she has been declared illegitimate. For this reason only the Duke of Cleves would not have her; and she was offered, with the insignificant dowry of thirty or forty thousand crowns, to Duke Philip of Bavaria.

The King, I consider, has resolved that she shall not marry out of the realm, for fear a claim should be made in her name to the crown, she being the only child whose legitimacy is recognised by the Church, and the Prince having been born since the schism from the Apostolic See.

Moreover, my lord, they cannot recall the Act of Parliament by which she was illegitimatized, without acknowledging the Pope's authority; and to this they will not condescend, if only because he would compel them to restore the property of the Church and the holy places which they have desecrated. Besides the danger of being called on for restitution, submission to the Pope would also be an evidence of great inconstancy; they have sent men of rank and note to the scaffold for maintaining the Papal authority; and to restore that authority would cause scandal and mistrust, and, possibly, tumult and sedition.

Marillac to Francis the First.

December 4, 1540.   [MS. Bibliot. Impér. Paris.]

The embassy has departed to the Emperor. The Bishop of Winchester is waiting at Calais and Guisnes, pretending that his boxes have not yet all crossed the water, and it is plain enough that he means to follow the Emperor into Germany.

There is more talk of the Duke of Suffolk going to Calais, as at one time was confidently expected. The arrangement is somehow at an end. Things seem quieter and more tranquil here than they appeared when I last wrote, and nothing is talked of except rejoicings and amusements. I, for one, have never seen the King in such good spirits or in so good a humour as he is at present. He has adopted a new rule of life. He rises in the morning between five and six; at seven he hears mass; and afterwards he rides till dinner, which is at ten A.M. He tells me that being so much in the country, and changing his place so often, he finds himself much better in health than in the winter, when he was residing in London.

Note G.

Eustace Chappuys to Charles the Fifth.

London, November 19, 1541. [Archives at Brussels.*]

SIRE,—The day before yesterday, the lord admiral sent, by one of my servants, to tell me that the Queen had confessed to an intrigue, before her marriage, with Master Derham who is in the Tower. The Privy Seal (Lord Russell) confirmed the account yesterday. In the three years that the affair lasted, they slept together more than eighty nights without word or talk of marriage between them.

It has been discovered lately that Master Culpepper, gentleman of the bedchamber to the King, has received love presents from her, and, within these two months, has been with her twice in private five or six hours at a time. Lady Rochfort acted as their go-between, and is also sent to the Tower.

When I asked the Privy Seal (Lord Russell) what the King meant to do in the matter, he told me that his Majesty would be more patient and merciful with her than people would suppose, and even than her own relations desired. He meant the Duke of Norfolk, who (God knows why) would have the Queen burnt. I do not know that as yet she has been sent to the Tower. There was a talk of putting her in a suppressed nunnery near Richmond, attended by four women and some men.

The Lady of Cleves, I am told, is delighted, and she is to come to Richmond (if she be not already there) to be nearer the King. On all accounts I thought best to say nothing about her to the Privy Seal till I should have a better opportunity when again at the Court.

The Princess has been sent away with the Prince, and all the other ladies have gone to their homes.

Eustace Chappuys to Charles the Fifth.

London, December 3.

SIRE,—The clerk of the council was sent to me on St. Andrew's day, with a message from the lords of the said council, that the next day Culpepper and Derham would be tried.

---

* This and the four following letters have been printed by M. Gachard, *Analectes Historiques*, vol. i. p. 237.

They begged that one of my people might be present, and the same desire was expressed to the ambassador of France, the Venetian secretary, and the minister of the Duke of Cleves, who is still here.

I sent a man to the trial. The King's council were all present, and after a long examination, which lasted full six hours, the said two gentlemen were found guilty, and sentenced to be quartered as traitors.

Derham confessed that he had been often with the Queen, before she was affianced or engaged to the King, and he said he did not know that he had done wrong, as there was a promise of marriage between them.

Culpepper denied positively that he had ever had to do with her, or had ever solicited her. She had importuned him, through Lady Rochfort, to give her a secret meeting at Lincoln, and she had told him then what she had before let him know through Lady Rochfort, that she was languishing and dying of love for him.

It is thought that they will be executed to-day.

Lady Rochfort would have been condemned at the same time were it not for a frenzy into which she fell three days after her arrest. She returns to herself at times, and the King sees that great pains are taken for her cure. The admiral's wife is with her, and she is attended by physicians; her recovery being desired, that she may be the subject afterwards of exemplary punishment.

The Queen remains at Sion, and it is thought that the King, to show his clemency, will take no further steps about her until the Estates of the Realm, which have been summoned, decide how it shall be.

The King has gone away somewhere in the neighbourhood to divert his thoughts; and people fancied he would pay a visit to the Lady of Cleves; but he has chosen another route, and, so far, I cannot perceive that he has any idea of taking her again.

The clerk of the council (Paget) having been long a friend of mine, I could not help saying to him that, if the King separated from his present Queen on the ground of her previous conduct, according to the common report in the Low Countries, he had equally good reason to part with the Lady of Cleves. He did not deny this . . . and he told me he did not think that the King would ever return to her, or that he would marry again at all unless the Parliament constrained him.

Eustace Chappuys to Charles the Fifth.

London, Jan. 29, 1542.

SIRE,—The session of Parliament, or of the Estates of the Realm, has just commenced. The chief point on which the chancellor dwelt in his opening speech was the crime committed by the Queen, of which he made the very worst possible.

The lords spiritual and temporal went into the business four days ago. They declared the Queen and Lady Rochfort guilty of high treason. The old Duchess of Norfolk and her daughter are sentenced to be imprisoned for life; and Lord William, his wife, and the other accomplices, also, for the same offence.

The resolution of the peers will be laid before the representatives of the people in two days.

At the very moment while I was writing the above, I was informed that the Commons House had this morning come to the same resolution about the Queen and the ladies, as the bishops and peers have done, and the Queen, it is to be feared, will be soon sent to the Tower. She is still at Syon, very cheerful and more plump and pretty than ever: she is as careful about her dress, she is as imperious and wilful, as at the time when she was with the King; notwithstanding that she expects to be put to death, that she confesses that she has well deserved it, and asks for no favour except that the execution shall be secret and not under the eyes of the world. Perhaps, if the King does not mean to marry again, he may show mercy to her; or if he find that he can divorce her on the plea of adultery, he may take another thus. The question, I am told, has been already debated among the learned theologians, although, so far, there is no appearance that the King thinks of any further marriage or of any other woman. The Lady of Cleves, as I understand, has less hope of a reconciliation than ever. She has sent the King a new-year's gift of certain pieces of velvet, and the King has presented her with some goblets and flagons.

Eustace Chappuys to Charles the Fifth.

Feb. 19, 1542.

SIRE,—In my letter of the 29th of January I informed your Majesty of the resolution taken by Parliament in the matter of the Queen and the ladies.

The King, from the time he had been informed of the said Queen's misconduct, had showed no signs of cheerfulness. Since the sentence he has recovered his spirits, and on the 29th he gave a supper and banquet to the ladies of the Court. There were twenty-six of them, with the lords, at his own table, and at a table adjoining there were thirty-five. The lady to whom for the time he was most attentive was the sister of Lord Cobham, and of the wife of Master Wyatt, lately divorced for adultery. She is a pretty young creature, with spirit enough, if she tries it, to play as bad a game as the others. He is said, also, to have a fancy for the daughter of Madame Albert, niece of the master of the horse, Sir Anthony Brown.*

Eustace Chappuys to Charles the Fifth.
Feb. 25, 1542.

SIRE,—In my letter of the 10th I informed your Majesty of all that had been done in the affair of the Queen; only I forgot to tell you that the King, after the vote of Parliament in her condemnation, wishing to proceed more humanely and more according to forms of law, sent some of his council with a deputation from the Houses to propose to her to come to the Parliament chamber to defend herself. She refused, however: she submitted herself to the King's mercy and good pleasure, and confessed that she had deserved to die.

Since that time, on the afternoon of the 10th, the Queen, after some resistance, and with some difficulty, was taken down the river to the Tower, preceded by a barge containing the Lord Privy Seal, several members of the council, and a number of servants. The Queen followed in a small close barge, with three or four men and as many women. The Duke of Suffolk came behind as a rear guard, in a large boat crowded with his retinue.

When they reached the Tower stairs, the lords disem-

---

* Henry, however, did not so easily forget Catherine Howard's conduct. On the 16th of April, Chappuys wrote:—
'There is no sign or hint that the King thinks of marrying again, either with the Lady of Cleves or any one else. Ever since the misconduct of his last wife he has become so sad and melancholy that he is altogether unlike himself. In every interview I have had with him I have found him full of sorrow, heaviness, and sighs.'
On the 15th of the following January Chappuys wrote again:—
'The King, from the time when he was made first aware of his last wife's wickedness, has been never anything but sad and pensive. He has shown no inclination for giving entertainments to ladies, or seeking their society.'

barked first, and afterwards the Queen, in a dress of black velvet. The same forms of respect were shown to her as when she was on the throne.

Two days after, being Sunday the 12th, in the evening, she was instructed to disburden her conscience; she was to die the following day. She desired that the block on which she was to be beheaded might be brought her, that she might learn how she was to place herself. This was done, and she made the experiment.

At seven o'clock the next morning, all the King's council, except the Duke of Suffolk, who was indisposed, and the Duke of Norfolk, presented themselves at the Tower, with a number of lords and gentlemen, amongst the rest being the Earl of Surrey, the Duke of Norfolk's son and the Queen's cousin. The Queen herself was shortly after beheaded, in the same place where Anne Boleyn suffered. A cloth was thrown over the body, which was taken away by some ladies, and Lady Rochfort was brought out, who seemed to be in a kind of frenzy till she died. Neither one nor the other said much, except to confess their misdeeds, and to pray for the King's welfare.

NOTE H.
Chappuys to the Emperor.

Jan. 10, 1539. [MS. Archives at Brussels.]

SIRE,—The 30th December now past, Lord Cromwell sent for the French ambassador, and entreated him, as the ambassador tells me, earnestly and anxiously, to write to the King his master to put a stop to the slanderous charges of heresy with which the King was defamed in France.

There was no cause or ground, Lord Cromwell said, for such accusations. The ambassador knew, and could himself see, that except in what concerned the Pope's authority, there was no innovation whatever. Religion and the Catholic faith remained inviolate.

Further, the King heard that he was accused of tyranny and cruelty, and that these things were said of him, not only by the vulgar and ignorant, but by some of the principal persons in France. The Cardinal of Paris, in the Most Christian King's own council, had talked vehemently to that effect, and no one had contradicted him or shown signs of being displeased.

The King thought this marvellously strange, and very little consonant with the good turns which he had done to the Most Christian King. He thought he had deserved to be spoken better of. He had not expected that they would have allowed his honour to be tainted without cause. The Prince who punished traitors by law, and under the forms of justice, did not deserve to be called cruel or tyrannical; and as to the execution of the Marquis of Exeter and his two accomplices, which seemed to have been the occasion of the report, the ambassador ought to know that their treason had been proved beyond all doubt since their death, by certain copies of letters to them from Cardinal Pole, as well as by other letters addressed by them to the cardinal. These copies, the originals of which had been burnt, were in the hands of the marchioness, and were found in a casket which she kept at the house of a confidential friend. In the same casket there were letters found of the late good Queen and of the Princess; and Lord Cromwell said it was quite certain that the marquis intended to usurp the crown at the King's death, to marry his son to the Princess, to despatch the Prince, and to destroy the family of the Seymours.

The marquis and marchioness had in time past worked upon the Princess, putting fancies into her head, and advising her to stand out against her father and disobey the law.

Lord Cromwell said too, that the marquis and his accomplices, or some one among them, must have had intelligence with me, and betrayed secrets of State to me; for they had many times found that your Majesty was informed of their most private intentions. The conspirators had been in communication, therefore, with me, or with some ambassador or agent of your Majesty, and these persons had carried messages between them and Cardinal Pole. He therefore begged the ambassador to write to the Most Christian King, and request that the defamations against the King might cease.

May it please your Majesty, the King himself, two days before, spoke to the French ambassador in the same language exactly, word for word, except only that he said nothing of the defamation of his character. Of the rest he omitted nothing, especially where it affected me.

Further, Lord Cromwell informed the ambassador that he had had the Bibles in English printed at Paris, which had cost him two thousand crowns, and which, when finished and paid for, had been arrested and sequestered by the university. This he considered very strange, and he required the ambassador to write for a release, and to assure the Most Christian King, on his behalf, that, if the release was granted at once, he would take it as a service which he would find means to recompense.

Thereupon, Sire, he went on to bid the ambassador tell him if there was a thing in the world which would increase and strengthen the alliance between their Majesties; and he said he could not fail to bring the King his master to consent to it, as well as to remove all causes and occasions which might at any time engender differences. He pressed the ambassador extremely to say if he could think of anything, and the ambassador conceives that Lord Cromwell wanted him to answer that, for the removal of all scruples, it would be well to abolish the pension which the King claims from France. The ambassador might be surprised, Lord Cromwell continued, at hearing such language from him, when language so unlike it had been used in time past. The King's bad ministers had been to blame, the Bishop of Winchester, Sir Francis Brian, and Sir Anthony Brown; and they were not rid of them yet. Before a year was over he hoped to speak in person with the Most Christian King, and to tell him things as much to his honour and profit as he had heard for a long time.

Sire, being at court afterwards, as the King was leaving his room to go to mass, he addressed himself to me. I told him I was come to wish him a happy new year, and I asked if he had any commands for me. He thanked me, saying that whenever I liked to come to see him I should be welcome; and thereupon he began to express his surprise at the delays about his marriage.*

Your Majesty had told his ambassador and Sir Philip Hoby, that the Queen Regent had full powers to settle everything. Your Majesty had sent her instructions so ample that she could not pretend that she had to consult you further; and he had not deserved, he said, to be trifled with and dissembled with on all sides, alluding to France. Notwithstanding your Majesty's words, the Queen persisted that she had insufficient authority, and he was forced to doubt whether she had that real desire for the completion of the affair which she affected to the English ambassador.

She was not to be excused, he said, for having neglected to communicate with the ambassador, after he had himself relinquished his demand for Milan. In the marriage of the Prin-

---

* With the Duchess of Milan.

cess Mary with Don Louis there might, perhaps, be difficulties; about his own there could be none.

To this, Sire, I replied, that he ought not to take it ill if her Highness could not come to a final resolution till she had received your Majesty's directions on more points than one. There was the state of Milan ; there was the French pension ; there was the dispensation for the affinity between himself and the Duchess of Milan ; and at the date of your Majesty's last letter, her courier had not reached you. Though he had given up his pretensions to Milan, your Majesty's pleasure had still to be ascertained about it. The dispensation was an unconsidered subject. The recovery of the pension was a new one, and had no natural connexion with the marriage ; and if there had been no other reason for delay, it was enough that he no longer contemplated the marriage of the Princess. It might well be a question with your Majesty whether you would allow one marriage without the other. Moreover, it might be that the Queen had heard that Duke Frederick was going to your Majesty, and before giving her answer she might have wished to know if a resolution had been arrived at touching the Danish succession. True, he had himself said that he did not care for any large settlement with the Duchess ; but your Majesty and the Queen were bound in honour to consider the children who might be born of the marriage. There was already a Prince who would succeed to the crown of England, and the Danish title might be of great importance to them.

He made me no answer, but left me, and I went to mass ; Lord Cromwell then joined me, and said he had news from Germany. The Estates, or at least part of them, he told me, were about to assemble at Cologne. By degrees he changed the subject, and said he marvelled at your Majesty's coldness about the marriage of his master with the Duchess of Milan. Your Majesty, he concluded, meant to give her to the Princes of Cleves and Lorraine.

That would be a pretty business, I replied, to give her to both, to gain two sons-in-law with one daughter. I told him your Majesty understood well enough the difference between his master and such connexions as those—only the conditions had to be looked to. He said nothing to that, but pretended he had some business to despatch, and left me for the usual reason, that he wished to avoid suspicion.

After dinner, Sire, the King began to talk to me of the wars which his Holiness was commencing. He said your

Majesty would not be pleased for a great many reasons. . . . .
Afterwards he returned to the marriage, and repeated part of
what he had said in the morning. He said that his subjects
were extremely importunate with him about taking a wife,
and his age did not allow him to delay too long. The French
boasted that your Majesty would not venture to conclude the
treaty without their consent, and this he supposed was the
real cause of the hesitation. A few days would show what
was to be looked for. Sire, I am unable to say how he will
act; but he seemed to me perplexed and thoughtful. He is
none the less vexed because it suits him to talk largely and
haughtily, and to treat the world as if they were sheep.

Every one tells me (and I am myself of the same opinion),
that he has a strong regard for the Duchess of Milan; and
three days ago, a gentleman who knows all his secrets told
me he would take her, if she came to him without a farthing.

As to the Princess's marriage, the French ambassador says
he has heard from good authority (though he may not
reveal his informant's name) that the King intends to give
her to the young Duke of Cleves, and to connect himself with
the King of Denmark, the Duke of Saxony and Prussia, and
the Landgrave of Hesse. He undertakes to find money for
them if they go to war with your Majesty. . . . . For myself,
I can believe that the King will be glad to make alliances
there and wherever he can, to defend himself against your
Majesty. He is not a man to go to sleep, and he will do his
best to find your Majesty in work elsewhere, that you may
have no leisure to meddle with him here. But I cannot
think that he will marry the Princess out of the realm. If it be
so, we shall soon know it, for the King is going in a few days
to see his son; and if he has any thought of the kind he will
not fail to speak to her on the subject. Suspecting or believing that the Dukes of Cleves and Lorraine are in communication with your Majesty about the Duchess of Milan, he
will endeavour to cross them by an offer of the Princess with
all the conditions which they can desire; and he knows well
that if he misses this chance with the Duchess, he will have
lost his last hope of returning to good terms with your Majesty. He is prepared for all contingencies, however. He is
collecting ammunition and materials for war, and within these
five days the master of the ordnance has been with me to take
leave, being sent down to the Scottish Borders to examine
the fortifications in the northern counties. Trusty persons
are on their way to Guisnes and Calais also, and to all parts

of the realm. The King has taken alarm at the transports which are collected in Flanders. Two or three times lately he has said to me that he could not conceive why those vessels should be taking on board ammunition and ordnance in Flanders, if they were meant for use in the Mediterranean. There must be enough of such things in Spain.

For general news here, Sire, on the last of December the master of the horse, Carew, was arrested and carried a prisoner to the Tower. Instantly that the order was issued for his arrest, officers were sent to take possession of his property; and people think the King will not forget to give directions to secure the beautiful diamonds, pearls, and numberless jewels he gave to the grand master's wife, the greater part of which were taken from the late good Queen.

As to the offices held by the said Carew, it seems that it was settled before his arrest how they should be distributed; for the order came out the following morning. Sir Anthony Brown is master of the horse, although it is not more than two days since Lord Cromwell spoke to the French ambassador of the ill offices which he had lately done in France, complaining that, like an arrogant blockhead, he had mixed his private quarrels and complaints with the affairs of his commission; the King had given him an honourable situation, but he should content himself with what he had got, without looking for more.

The evidence against Carew, people tell me, is a letter found in the marchioness's casket, giving her information of things which had been discussed in the King's private room. Since his imprisonment, he has been pressed to confess something against the marquis. It seems the evidence of young Pole was not enough; and these people will follow the Carinthian practice—execution first, and process after. As to the copies of letters which the King and Cromwell pretended to have found in a casket, among them being letters of mine, I cannot tell what these letters could be. I never wrote a letter to any person in the realm that I should care to see published, unless it were to the late good Queen and the Princess; and anything written to them must have been burned immediately.

The marquis and the others who were executed, were charged, and heavily charged, because no letters were found. They had received letters, and it was pretended that they were burned, because they would have compromised them. For myself, I have many times written to the Princess, to

advise her not to expose herself to suspicion. I have sent
her a dozen letters, which she has to show if necessary, and I
should be glad if anything was to make the King ask for
them and read them.

To return to the master of the horse. I have been given
to understand that, in hopes of pardon, he has discovered
various things affecting both himself and the marquis. Nothing, however, has been specified, except that when the
master of the horse brought news to the marquis that the late
Queen Jane was delivered of a male child, the marquis was
much vexed. If this was true, it could only be from the love
and affection which he bore towards the Princess, in whose
service he would gladly have shed his blood, as he often sent
to me to say.

If any letter of the master of the horse was found among
the marchioness's papers, it must have been about something
that concerned the Princess, to whom he was always himself most devoted. It seems they wish to leave her as few such
friends as possible. However, notwithstanding the fine presents your Majesty made the said master of the horse when
he came to swear to the peace, he has always inclined towards
France. The good Edward Neville many times reproached
him for it.

As to interceding with the King in behalf of young Pole,
I think, for the considerations mentioned in my other letters,
your Majesty has acted with your accustomed prudence in
abstaining from interference. There was good reason for remaining passive, and the execution since that time of his eldest
brother, makes one inclined to desist from saying anything.
People tell me that his life will be spared, but that he will
remain in perpetual prison. I was informed that in Christmas
week he tried to smother himself with a cushion.

Sire, this morning, as I was melting the wax to seal this letter,
the French ambassador's secretary came to me with a message
from his master. Lord Cromwell, returning late yesterday
from the Court, passed the ambassador's house, and went in
to tell him that two hours previously the King had received
letters from the Court of France, informing him that the Most
Christian King had imprisoned two Franciscans for defaming
the King of England in their sermons. The Franciscans were to
be severely punished; and on the first day of the year the Most
Christian King gave a grand entertainment to the English
ambassador.

Orders had been given also for the release of the printed

sheets of the Bible; and this news had marvellously delighted the King. He declared himself under great obligations to the Most Christian King, and to the French ambassador as well, for his many good offices in perpetuating the alliance between the Most Christian King and himself.

The said ambassador, however, desired that I should be told that all that had been done in France was an artifice only to deceive the English into confidence; and that he had himself in his own letters directed the measures which had been taken, or, at all events, those which affected the defamation and the sequestration of the Bibles.

The said ambassador desired also to know if it was true that the King of England had presented the Duchess of Milan with a diamond worth 60,000 ducats, as the world said. I told him it was the first that I had heard of it, as indeed it was.

London, Jan. 9, 1539.

Note I.

The Irish chiefs, who, as long as France was at enmity with England, had sought the support of the Court of Paris, transferred their allegiance to the Empire on the agitation of the divorce of Queen Catherine. Charles the Fifth endeavoured to frighten Henry into giving way, by fomenting sedition among his subjects. The Irish did not wait to be sought, but placed themselves and their swords, of their own accord, at the Emperor's feet. In the winter of 1528-9, the Earl of Desmond wrote, with offers of service, to Charles the Fifth, who was then at Toledo. Charles replied by sending his chaplain Gonzalo Fernandez, to see whether Desmond's powers were equal to his promises.

Instructions for Gonzalo Fernandez sent by us to Ireland to the Earl of Desmond.

Feb. 24, 1529. [MS. Archives at Brussels.]

Seeing that you, Gonzalo Fernandez, Chaplain of my Court, are going to Ireland to the Earl of Desmond, to open negotiations with the said earl in our behalf, your instructions are as follows:—

First, you will use all diligence to arrive at the place where the earl resides; and after presenting your credentials, you shall say to him that, inasmuch as one of his followers, named

Godfrey, has within these few days brought a letter to us, signifying a desire on the part of the said earl to be our ally and confederate, and with all his vassals and subjects to be friend of our friends and enemy of our enemies; and inasmuch as the said earl desires that we would send some confidential person who might learn his intentions, and see and report upon his resources; conformably with his request, we have sent you to speak with him; and in accepting his offer of goodwill, you shall tell him that he shall ever find in us a like disposition, and that he may hold himself assured of all the support which it may be in our power to give him.

You shall inform yourself of the force which the earl, with his friends, can command; and you shall desire him to explain in writing his expectations and plans, and to let us know what he will be able to effect against our common enemy.

The earl requests, further, that in case he declare openly for us, and we come hereafter to make peace with the King of England, we will not leave him uncomprehended in our treaty. You shall say that we have ever desired to be on good terms with the King of England. Our predecessors and his predecessors, our subjects and his subjects, have hitherto been friends and allies. We have ourselves borne an especial affection towards the English nation, and, for our own part, we have done all that lay in our power to remain at peace with the King. Notwithstanding, as is notorious to all the world, he has declared against us in favour of our enemy the King of France. He has given ear to evil and accursed advisers, who have persuaded him to separate from the Queen, our aunt, his lawful wife, and he has given the vice-royalty of Ireland to his bastard son.

This his conduct we have been unable to endure with patience. He has placed himself at enmity with God and the constitution of our Holy Mother Church. He has caused a scandal among all good princes and faithful Christians. He has injured the Queen, our aunt, and prejudiced the rights of the Princess, his only daughter and heiress of the realm; and things are now at such a point, that we are resolved to oppose him by all means in our power. We are assured that the said earl will join us, as he has proposed, with all the force which he can raise, and will assist us now and ever against our enemies.

You may assure him, further, that we will make no treaty with the King of England, in which he shall not be comprehended; and he, his friends, and subjects, shall ever find us fulfilling towards them the part of a faithful ally and confederate.

Done at Toledo, Feb. 24, 1529.

Report of Gonzalo Fernandez.
April 28, 1529.

On arriving at the coast of Ireland we touched at a port belonging to the King of England named Cork. Many of the Irish people came on board the ship, and told me that the gentleman of the Earl of Desmond had just returned from Spain with presents from the Emperor to the earl.

Leaving Cork, we were driven by bad weather into another harbour called Beran,* from whence I sent one of my servants to inform the earl of my arrival. In four days the earl's answer came, telling me that I was welcome, and that he was at a place called Dingle, where he hoped to see me. He addressed his letter to me as 'Chaplain of *our* Sovereign Lord the Emperor;' and this, I understand, is his usual mode of expression when speaking of his Majesty. He had also sent to some of the other noblemen of the country, with whom he proposed to form a league, to tell them of my arrival.

I set out again, and on the way five of the earl's people came to me to say that their master had gone to a harbour a few miles off to capture some French and English vessels there, and would be glad of my assistance. This I declined, and the earl, I understand, was satisfied with my excuses.

The day after, the 21st of April, we reached the said harbour of Dingle, and were honourably received by the townspeople, and by a party of the earl's attendants. About four o'clock the earl returned himself, attended by fifty horse and as many halberdiers. He came at once to my quarters, and asked after the welfare of 'our Lord the Emperor.' I replied that, by the grace of God, his Majesty was well, and I had sent his commendations to his lordship.

We then dined; and afterwards the earl and his council repaired to my chamber, where we presented him with his Majesty's letter. He read it and his council read it. His Majesty, he said, referred him to me. I was commissioned to make known his Majesty's pleasure to him. I at once declared my instructions, first in English to the earl, and afterward in Latin to his council; which I said were to this effect.

---

* Beerhaven, perhaps.

'One Godfrey, a friend of their lord, had lately presented
'himself to the Emperor with their lord's letter, in which their
'lord, after speaking of the goodwill and affection which he
'entertained towards the Emperor's Majesty, had expressed a
'desire to enter into close alliance with his Majesty, as friend
'to friend and enemy to enemy, declaring himself ready, in all
'things and at all times, to obey his Majesty's commands.

'Further, the said Godfrey had requested the Emperor to
'send a confidential person to Ireland, to learn more particu-
'larly their lord's intentions, and his resources and power; and
'further, to negotiate a treaty and establish a firm and complete
'alliance. For these purposes the Emperor commissioned my-
'self. I was the bearer to them of his Majesty's thanks for
'their proposals, and I said I was so far in my master's confi-
'dence that I was assured their lord might expect all possible
'assistance at the Emperor's hands.'

When I had done, the earl spoke a few words to his council.
He then took off his cap, and said he thanked his Majesty for
his gracious condescension. He had addressed himself to his
Majesty as to his sovereign lord, to entreat his protection.
His Majesty was placed in this world in his high position, in
order that no one prince might oppress or injure another. He
related his descent to me. He said that, between his family
and the English, there had ever existed a mortal enmity, and
he explained the cause to me.

I replied that his Majesty never failed to support his allies
and his subjects, and should he claim assistance in that capacity, his Majesty would help him as he helped all his other
good friends. I advised the earl to put in writing the words
which he had used to me. He thought it would be enough if
I repeated them; but when I said the story was too long, and
my memory might not retain it with accuracy, he said he
would do as I desired.

We then spoke of the support for which he was looking, of
his projects and resources, and of the places in which he proposed to serve. He said he wanted from his Majesty four
large vessels, two hundred tons each, six pinnaces well provided with artillery, and five hundred Flemings to work them.
I said at once and earnestly, that such a demand was out of all
reason, before he, on his part, had achieved something in his
Majesty's service. I remonstrated fully and largely, although,
to avoid being tedious, I omit the details. In the end his
council were satisfied that he must reduce his demands till his
Majesty had more reason to know what was to be expected
from him, and he consented, as will be seen by his own memoir.

Of all men in the world the earl hates most deeply the Cardinal of York. He told me he had been in alliance with France, and had a relation called De Quindel, now with the French army in Italy. In future, he said he would have no dealings with the French. As your Majesty's enemies, they were his enemies.

Your Majesty will be pleased to understand that there are in Ireland four principal cities. The city of Dublin is the largest and richest in the island, and neither in the town nor in the neighbourhood has the Earl of Desmond land or subjects. The Earl of Kildare is sovereign in that district, but that earl is a kinsman of the Earl of Desmond, and has married his cousin.

The Earl of Kildare, however, is at present a prisoner in the Tower of London.

Of the other three cities, one is called Waterford, the second Cork, the third Limerick; and in all of these the Earl of Desmond has lordships and vassals. He has dominions, also, among the wild tribes; he has lords and knights on his estates who pay him tribute. He has some allies, but not so many, by a great deal, as he has enemies.

He has ten castles of his own, some of which are strong and well built, especially one named Dungarvan, which the King has often attempted to take without success.

The earl himself is from thirty to forty years old, and is rather above the middle height. He keeps better justice throughout his dominions than any other chief in Ireland. Robbers and homicides find no mercy, and are executed out of hand. His people are in high order and discipline. They are armed with short bows and swords. The earl's guard are in mail from neck to heel, and carry halberds. He has also a number of horse, some of whom know how to break a lance. They all ride admirably without saddle or stirrup.

After the report of Gonzalvo Fernandez, Desmond himself continues in Latin.

Hereunto be added informations addressed to the invincible and most sacred Cæsar, ever august, by the Earl of Desmond, Lord of Ogonyll and the liberties of Kilcrygge.

I, James Earl of Desmond, am of royal blood, and of the race of the Conqueror who did lawfully subdue Britain, great and small, and did reduce Scotland and Ireland under his yoke.

The first cause of the enmity between myself and the King of England is an ancient prophecy or prediction, believed by the English nation, and written in their books and chronicles, that all England will be conquered by an Earl of Desmond, which enterprise I have not yet undertaken.

The second cause is that, through fear of this prophecy, the King of England has committed his powers to my predecessors who have borne rule in Ireland ; and when Thomas Earl of Desmond, my grandfather, in peaceable manner attended Parliament in Ireland, no cause being alleged against him, but merely in dread of the prophecy, they struck off his head.

The third cause is that, when Richard, son of the King of England [*sic*], heard that there were ancient feuds between the English and my predecessors, he came to Ireland with an army and a great fleet in the time of my father ; and then did my father make all Ireland to be subdued unto himself, some few towns only excepted.

The fourth cause is that, by reason of the aforesaid feuds, the King of England did cause Gerald Earl of Kildare, my father's kinsman, to be destroyed in prison [*destrui in car-ceribus*] until that my father, by might and power, did liberate the said Earl of Kildare, and did obtain his own purposes, and did make his kinsman viceroy of Ireland.

The fifth cause is that, when peace was hardly begun between my aforesaid father and the King of England, a certain sickness fell upon my father, I myself being then eight years old.

The King, when he heard this, made a league of Irish and English to kill my father ; he being then, as they thought, unable to take the field. They, being banded together, made war against my father for twenty-four years, wherein, by God's grace, they had small success.

The sixth cause is that, when peace was made at last between the King that now is and myself, I, in faith of the said peace, sent certain of my servants to the parts beyond the seas to Flanders and France, and the attorneys of the King of England did despoil my servants of the sum of 9000*l*., and threw them into prison, where they now remain.

Hereon follows my supplication :—

These things premised, I, the aforesaid earl, do implore and entreat the invincible and most sacred Majesty of Cæsar Augustus that he will deign to provide me with remedy, and I, with all my horses and people, do devote myself to your Majesty's service, seeing that your Majesty is appointed for the welfare of the oppressed, and to be lord paramount of all the earth.

To revenge the injuries done to myself and my family by the King of England, I have the following powers ; that is to

NOTE I.

say, 16,500 foot and 1500 horse. Also I have friends, confederate with me, whose names be these—

1. The Prince O'Brien, who can make 600 horse and 1000 foot.
2. Trobal de Burgh ,, 100 ,, 600 ,,
3. Sir Richard Poer ,, 40 ,, 200 ,,
4. Lord Thomas Butler ,, 60 ,, 240 ,,
5. Sir John Galty ,, 80 ,, 400 ,,
6. Sir Gerald Fitzgerald ,, 40 ,, 200 ,,
7. The White Knight ,, 400 ,, 800 ,,
8. O'Donnell, Prince of Ulster ,, 800 ,, 4000 ,,
9. The Knight of the Valley ,, 40 ,, 240 ,,
10. Baron MacMys ,, 40 ,, 500 ,,
11. Captain Macguire ,, 30 ,, 200 ,,

With divers others whose names be here omitted.

Moreover, I, the aforesaid James Earl of Desmond, do make known to the Majesty of Cæsar august, that there is an alliance between me and the King of Scotland, and, by frequent embassies, we understand each other's purposes and intentions.

Finally, divine grace permitting, I intend to gather together my own and my friends' powers, and lead them in person against Piers Butler, deputy of the King of England, and against Limerick, Wexford, and Dublin, the cities which the King holds in Ireland.

For the aid for which I look from your Majesty, I desire especially cannon available for land service and fit for breaching castles. May it please your Majesty, therefore, to send me cannon, that I may be the better able to do your Majesty service.

And for myself, I promise on my faith to obey your Majesty in all things. I will be friend of your friends; enemy of your enemies; and your Majesty's especial and particular subject. If ever I chance to displease you, I will submit myself to your correction and chastisement.

Written in my town, this 28th day of April, 1529, in the presence of Gonzalvo Fernandez, Denys Mac D——c Doctor of Arms and Medicine, Denys Tathe, Maurice Herly.

JAMES OF DESMOND.

Five years later, at the outbreak of Lord Thomas Fitzgerald's rebellion, another application was made to the Emperor for assistance.

Corn O'Brien, Prince of Ireland, to the Emperor Charles V.
July 21, 1534. [MS. Archives at Brussels.]

To the most sacred and most invincible Cæsar, Charles Emperor of the Romans, Most Catholic King of Spain, health with all submission.—Most sacred Cæsar, lord most clement, we give your Majesty to know that our predecessors for a long time quietly and peacefully occupied Ireland, with constancy, force, and courage, and without rebellion. They possessed and governed this country in manner royal, as by our ancient chronicles doth plainly appear. Our said predecessors and ancestry did come from your Majesty's realm of Spain, where they were of the blood of a Spanish prince, and many Kings of that lineage, in long succession, governed all Ireland happily, until it was conquered by the English. The last King of this land was of my blood and name; and ever since that time our ancestors, and we ourselves, have ceased not to oppose the English intruders; we have never been subject to English rule, or yielded up our ancient rights and liberties; and there is at this present, and for ever will be, perpetual discord between us, and we will harass them with continual war.

For this cause, we, who till this present, have sworn fealty to no man, submit ourselves, our lands, our families, our followers, to the protection and defence of your Majesty, and of free will and deliberate purpose we promise to obey your Majesty's orders and commands in all honest behests. We will serve your Majesty with all our force; that is to say, with 1660 horse and 2440 foot, equipped and armed. Further, we will levy and direct for your Majesty's use 13,000 men, well armed with harquebuss, bows, arrows, and swords. We will submit to your Majesty's will and jurisdiction more than a hundred castles, and they and all else shall be at your Majesty's disposition to be employed as you shall direct.

We can undertake also for the assistance and support of our good brother the Earl of Desmond, whose cousin, the daughter of the late Earl James, your Majesty's friend, is our wife.

Our further pleasure will be declared to you by our servants and friends, Robert and Dominic de Paul, to whom your Majesty will deign to give credence. May your Majesty be ever prosperous.

Written at our Castle at Clare, witness, our daughter, July 21, 1534, by your humble servant and unfailing friend,

CORNY O'BRIEN, Prince of Ireland.

THE END.

www.ingramcontent.com/pod-product-compliance
Lightning Source LLC
Chambersburg PA
CBHW020242170426
43202CB00008B/192